Yvain

Yvain
The Knight of the Lion

Chrétien de Troyes
Translated from the Old French
by Burton Raffel
Afterword by Joseph J. Duggan

Yale University Press
New Haven and London

Designed by Nancy Ovedovitz and set in Garamond
No. 3 type by Brevis Press. Printed in the United
States of America by Vail-Ballou Press, Binghamton,
New York.

Library of Congress Cataloging-in-Publication Data

Chrétien, de Troyes, 12th cent.
    Yvain, the Knight of the Lion.
    Bibliography: p. 227
    1. Ywain (Legendary character)—Romances.
I. Raffel, Burton. II. Title.
PQ1447.E5R34   1987   841'.1   86–23346
ISBN 0–300–03837–2 (alk. paper)

The paper in this book meets the guidelines for per-
manence and durability of the Committee on Produc-
tion Guidelines for Book Longevity of the Council on
Library Resources.

10 9 8 7 6 5 4 3 2 1

for Eli Sagan,
of course

Contents

Translator's Preface

My basic text has been Chrestien de Troyes, *Yvain: Le Cheva-lier au Lion* (Manchester, England: Manchester University Press, 1967), incorporating the critical text of Wendelin Foerster and with an introduction, notes, and glossary by T. B. W. Reid. I have sometimes disagreed with both Foerster and Reid as to matters of punctuation, and less often as to the precise meaning of a particular disputed passage. Two volumes I found absolutely indispensable are A.-J. Greimas, *Dictionnaire de l'ancien français, jusqu'au milieu du XIVe siècle* (Paris: Larousse, 1980) and Frédéric Godefroy, *Lexique de l'ancien français,* ed. J. Bonnard and Am. Salmon (Paris: Champion, 1976). I sometimes drew upon (and always enjoyed) William W. Kibler's beautifully written and sensitively conceived *An Introduction to Old French* (New York: The Modern Language Association of America, 1984).

The most important decision for anyone translating a poem like *Yvain* is formal: what does one do, in Modern English, with Chrétien's octosyllabic rhyming couplets? His metre is plainly an impossible one for the English version of a poem of 6,818 lines. (For comparative purposes, note that *Beowulf* has 3,182 lines, and the *Odyssey* roughly 12,000.) The closest formal equivalent, iambic tetrameter, would be more than risky. One necessarily tends, given the physical constraints of the measure, to place the caesura after every second foot. The great strength of iambic pentameter, never more fully demonstrated than in the end-stopped couplets of Alexander Pope, is that the caesura not only can never be placed in the exact middle of the line, there being indeed no exact middle available in a line of five rather than of four metrical feet, but that the greater length of the iambic pentameter line encourages placement of the caesura after the first, second, third, or fourth foot—and also permits use of more than one caesura in a line. Two marked metrical pauses would annihilate an iambic tetrameter line, which as I say naturally and almost inevitably tends to break at the midpoint. This makes iambic tetrameter excessively even, often monotonous, and especially monotonous at any length greater than that of a short lyric. Not surprisingly, in this century it is a metre that has been little used, even in shorter poems. The only modern poet to make extensive use of iambic tetrameter is AE (George William Russell). The best-informed and fairest critic of twentieth-century English and American poetry, David Perkins, rightly says that "the poetry of Russell is inadequate to its theme, but in his case the trouble is not his experience, which was surely genuine, but his lack of technical and imaginative . . . skill" (*A History of Modern Poetry: From the 1890s to the High Modernist Mode* [Cambridge, Mass.: Harvard University Press, 1976], p. 256). Metre is neither the beginning nor the end of Russell's limitations, but it is a significant part of them.

Rhyme is an equally difficult matter. Not only is French considerably more rhyme-rich than is English, but it is also a syllable-timed' rather than a stress-timed language. French prosody is therefore syllabic, while both the native form of English prosody—employed in the poetry composed during the Old English period, including *Beowulf*—and the combination of stress and syllable-count prosody worked out in England in the centuries after the Norman Conquest, rely heavily on stress patterns. Milton could argue against, and

dispense with, the use of rhyme for his *Paradise Lost*. No
French poet either could or did make the same argument or
follow the same practice.

And both metre and rhyme played poetic roles, for Chré-
tien, that they play no longer. Chrétien wrote his poetry; it
is not oral verse in the sense that Homer's and much of Old
English poetry have been shown to be. But like the other
poets of his time, Chrétien regularly recited his poetry to
the courtly audiences for whom it was written (as indeed *Au-
cassin et Nicolette*, perhaps half a century later, was alterna-
tively recited, in its prose portions, and sung, in its poetic
portions). "Since we lack access to native speakers of Old
French," as Kibler drily observes, "we cannot hope to acquire
a perfect understanding of its pronunciation." But we do
know that "There was word stress (as in modern English)
rather than only sentence stress (characteristic of modern
French)" (Kibler, pp. 8–9). The movement of Chrétien's
verse, accordingly, is both designed for a distinctly colloquial
mode and, in certain of its linguistic features, closer to
English than the verse of, say, Racine or Baudelaire or Clau-
del. It is distinctly speech-like in syntax and lexicon. Rhym-
ing octosyllabic couplets nicely carried those qualities, for
Chrétien; they would not do the same for modern English or
for modern English readers.

Vers libre (free verse), though it has become the prevailing
prosody of our time, is not truly suitable as an equivalent to
Chrétien's couplets. The medieval concept of a quasi-epic ro-
mance requires an underlying formal prosodic regularity, a
continuing sense for the audience (hearer or reader) of a rea-
sonably uniform measure which can tie together an often epi-
sodic structure. To approximate Chrétien's verse movement
and tone as closely as I could, I have therefore devised a flex-
ible line of an invariable three stresses, but with varying
numbers of unstressed syllables. In practice, this measure
varies from an extreme of four total syllables to the opposite

extreme of thirteen total syllables. A quick but probably
largely accurate count reveals only five instances of these ex-
tremes, lines 4346, 5180, and 6341 having four total sylla-
bles, and lines 5855 and 5987 having thirteen total syllables.
Only line 4632 has twelve total syllables. The vast majority
of the lines in this translation are clustered within a range of
six to nine syllables. The measure seems to me—and more
importantly, seems to the scholars whose advice and criticism
I have sought, notably Ronnie Apter, John Miles Foley, and
Alexandra H. Olsen—to adapt well to the pace and to the
moods of Chrétien's measure.

The function of rhyme in a poem intended primarily for
the ear, rather than for the eye, does not seem reproducible
in modern English. Nor does rhyme seem either necessary,
given the changed literary conditions of our era, or useful,
given (as Milton declares in the prefatory note to *Paradise
Lost*) that "Rime [is] no necessary Adjunct or true Ornament
of Poem or good Verse, in longer works especially." As he
adds, poets who have used rhyme have been obliged "much
to thir own vexation, hindrance, and constraint to express
many things otherwise, and for the most part worse than else
they would have exprest them." Three hundred and more
years after Milton wrote those indignant sentences, we no
longer need to claim "an ancient liberty recover'd to Heroic
Poem from the troublesom and modern bondage of Riming."

This brief preface is not intended as either a historical or a
critical statement. I should note, however, that the transla-
tion was undertaken because Chrétien is a great and influen-
tial poet who has been virtually nonexistent in English.
Further, *Yvain* can be considered his masterpiece. It is fully
as impressive as, though of course different from, such well-
known twelfth-century works as *Le Chanson de Roland* and *La
Poema de Mio Cid*. Those poems have been fortunate enough
to find not only one but several superbly capable translators.
Chrétien in general, and *Yvain* in particular, have not been

so fortunate. It has been my hope to remedy a situation patently out of balance, and I will be content if this translation allows the modern English reader some reasonably clear view of Chrétien's swift, clear style, his wonderfully inventive storytelling, his perceptive characterizations and sure-handed dialogue, his racy wit and sly irony, and the vividness with which he evokes, for us as for his twelfth-century audiences, the emotions and the values of a flourishing, vibrant world. Chrétien is a delight to read—and to translate.

Acknowledgments

In addition to the scholars already mentioned, I am deeply grateful to Professor Joseph J. Duggan, of the University of California at Berkeley, for agreeing to read through the entire translation with one of the most practiced and knowledgeable eyes in the literary world, for supplying the afterword, and for supplying the bibliography.

My largest debt, which is expressed in very brief form in the dedication, is to Eli Sagan, a distinguished psychosociologist who had the wit to put together Chrétien and myself and whose support in making the translation was literally indispensable.

B. R.

Yvain
The Knight of the Lion

Chrétien de Troyes

Artus, li buens rois de Bretaingne,
La cui proesce nos ansaingne,
Que nos soiiens preu et cortois . . .

Arthur, good king of Brittany,
Whose knighthood teaches us
To be courteous, to be true knights,
Held court as a king should
On that holy day always   5
Known as the Pentecost.
The king was at Carlisle, in Wales.
And after eating in those rooms
The knights gathered there
Where the ladies called them,   10
And the young ladies, too, and the girls.
Some gossiped, told and retold
Stories, some spoke of love,
The anguish and the sadness of Love
And its glories, as Love's disciples   15
And followers knew them, then
When Love flourished, and was rich.
But today Love is almost
Deserted, its followers fallen
Away, its worshippers gone.   20
For those who practiced Love
Could truly call themselves courtiers—
Noble, generous, honorable.
Love has turned into silly
Stories, told by liars   25
Who feel nothing, know nothing, all talk
And empty boasts, dishonesty
And vanity and windy noise.
How much better to speak of those dead

3

And gone than bother with the living!   30
Better a courtier, dead,
Than a vulgar peasant, alive.
I prefer to tell a tale
Worth hearing of a king so famous
That men still speak of him, near   35
And far, for the Bretons have told
His story truly: asleep
Or awake, he is famous forever.
And thinking of him we think
Of those blessed knights, chosen   40
To struggle for honor at his side.
    And that day those knights were astonished
At the king, who rose and left them.
And many knights were deeply
Insulted, and said so, angrily,   45
For no one had ever seen him
Rise from a feast and go
To his bedroom, to rest or to sleep.
But that day he did, and the queen
Kept him, and he stayed so long   50
Beside her that he forgot himself,
And forgot his knights, and slept.
    Sitting outside his door
Were Sagremor and Kay
And Dodinel and Gawain   55
And also lord Yvain,
And also Calgrenant,
A handsome knight who'd begun
Telling them a story—not praising
Himself, but a tale of disgrace.   60
And as he told his tale
The queen could hear him, and got up
From beside the sleeping king
And came out among them so quietly

That before they knew she was there   65
She appeared in their midst, and only
Calgrenant, and no one else,
Rose to his feet in her honor.
And Kay, with his slashing tongue,
Savage and nasty, snarled: 70
    "By God, Calgrenant!
What a prancing courtier you've become—
How nice to see you so gallant,
Surely the best of us all.
And you think so, too, don't you,   75
In that empty skull. Oh, you do,
You do. How fitting for my lady
To find you more courteous than any
Of us, and a better knight.
We couldn't be bothered to rise,   80
I suppose; we're all too lazy
—Or maybe we just didn't care!
By God, sir, we never
Saw my lady until
You stood. That's all that happened."   85
    "Now Kay," said the queen, "I think
You'd burst, you really would,
If you couldn't spill out that poisonous
Spite you're always full of.
How mean and ugly, how base,   90
To slander your friends like this."
    "My lady!" said Kay. "If we haven't
Gained by your presence, allow us,
Please, not to lose. I hardly
Believe I've spoken a word   95
I need to be scolded for. Please!
I beg you, say no more.
There's neither sense nor courtesy
In preserving a foolish quarrel.

Such words should stop right here;   100
Let no one make more of them. Grumbling
Be done: command our story
Teller to finish, now,
The tale he'd already begun."
    And Calgrenant spoke up,   105
Answering Kay's remarks:
    "Sir! If there's been a quarrel
It means little or nothing to me.
And why should I be bothered?
You may have been insulting,   110
But no harm's been done. My dear
Sir Kay! You've said such things,
And often, to better men,
And wiser, than me. Insulting
Others is a habit with you.   115
Manure will always stink,
And horseflies bite, and bees
Buzz, and bores be boring.
But excuse me, my lady, grant me
Your leave to leave off my story.   120
I beg you, please, not to speak
Of it again, nor give me,
By your grace, so unwelcome an order."
    "My lady!" said Kay. "Everyone
Here would be grateful to hear him.   125
We all wish him to go on.
Don't do it simply for me!
But by the faith you owe the king,
Your lord and mine, you'd do well
To order him on, make him   130
Continue."
    "Calgrenant!"
Said the queen. "Don't let yourself worry
Over insults from our Lord Steward Kay!

He's so used to speaking wickedness
One can hardly even scold him.   135
I order you, and also implore you,
Not to be angry on his
Account, nor to keep from telling us
Anything pleasant, because
Of him. If you wish my love,   140
Tell it again, from the start!"
    "God knows, oh lady, what a terribly
Painful demand you make of me.
I'd rather have one of my eyes
Plucked out than go on with my story,   145
Except that I fear your anger,
And so I do what pleases you
However unpleasant I find it.
But since you wish it, listen!
Give me your ears and your mind!   150
The spoken word is lost
If your heart and your mind can't hear it.
There are men, I assure you, who listen
Happily and hear nothing,
Men little more than ears,   155
Their brains distant, detached.
Words can come to the ear
Like blowing wind, and neither
Stop nor remain, just passing
By, like fleeting time,   160
If hearts and minds aren't awake,
Aren't ready and willing to receive them.
Only the heart can take them
In, and hold them, and keep them.
The ears are a road, a door,   165
For the voice to reach the heart,
And hearts accept the voice
In themselves, though it comes through the ear.

So anyone who truly hears me,
Give me your ears and your minds,   170
For my tale has nothing to do
With dreams, or fables, or lies,
Like so many others have offered,
But only what I saw myself.

It was almost seven years   175
Ago, I was lonely as a peasant
And hunting after adventure,
Fully armed, exactly
As a knight ought to be, and I came
To a road on my right-hand side,   180
In the middle of a deserted forest.
It was a treacherous path, full
Of brambles, choked with thorns.
For all its obstacles, despite
The effort, I followed that road.   185
And for almost the rest of the day
I drove my horse along
That path, until at last
I came out of Brocelande forest.
And then I rode over open   190
Fields and saw a tower,
Half a Welsh mile distant,
Or even less, but not more.
Pacing my horse, I came
To the outer wall and the moat,   195
Deep and wide all around,
And saw, standing on the bridge,
He whose castle it was,
A hunting hawk on his hand.

I'd barely greeted him when he stepped   200
Forward and grasped my stirrups
And suggested I dismount. And I did.
There was no point pretending, for plainly
I needed shelter. And he told me
A hundred times over, and more,   205
That whatever road led me
To his home was a blessed path.
And thus we crossed the bridge
And came through the gate and into
The courtyard. And there in the middle   210
Of his courtyard the lord of the castle
—To whom may God on high
Repay the honor and the happiness
He gave me that night—had hung
A gong, not hammered of iron,   215
Nor carved of wood, but cast
In copper, and he struck it three times
With a mallet tied to a post.
And all his household, who had been
Inside, hearing that sound,   220
And hearing his voice, came down
And came out of his house, and hurried
Into the courtyard. And some
Took my horse from that courteous lord,
Who was still holding it, and led it   225
Away. And I saw coming toward me
A young and beautiful girl.
I watched with great interest: she was tall
And slim and held herself well.
And quickly, deftly she helped me   230
Out of my armor, and draped
Around me a short cloak,
Peacock blue, fur-trimmed,
And the rest of them left and left us

Alone together, not a soul   235
In sight, which pleased me: there was nothing
Else I'd rather have seen.
Then she led me to the loveliest lawn
In the world, fenced all around
With a wall, and sat me down.   240
I found her wonderfully well-bred,
Her words so well-chosen, and well-taught,
And she so charming, so delightful,
That I felt myself filled with pleasure
And hoped I might never again   245
Need to move. But darkness
Betrayed me, night came, and the lord
Of the castle came to find me,
For the time to dine had come.
I could hardly object, or delay,   250
And I went as he wished, at once.
But that supper too went
As I wanted, for she sat across from me,
Which made everything well. And after
That meal the lord of the castle   255
Told me he could not remember
How long it had been since he'd sheltered
A wandering knight, a true
Knight errant, truly in search
Of adventure, though over the years   260
He'd sheltered many a knight.
And then he asked, in return
For hospitality, if I
Would return to his house, if I could.
And I said, "Of course, dear sir!"   265
In honor, what else could I possibly
Say? Deny so small
A favor to so gracious a host?

I was very well lodged, that night,
And as soon as one could see   270
The morning light, my horse
Was ready, exactly as I'd asked
The night before. I blessed
My host and his lovely daughter
In the name of the Holy Spirit,   275
And took my leave of them all
As soon as I could. I hadn't
Gotten far from that castle
When I came to a clearing full
Of wild bulls, savage beasts   280
Fighting among themselves
And making so loud a noise,
And beasts so fierce and so reckless
That even the sight of them would make you
Afraid. And I was, and retreated,   285
For no animal alive is as fierce
And as dangerous as a bull. And I saw,
Sitting on a tree stump, a lowborn
Creature, black as a Moor,
Huge, and hideously ugly   290
—Indeed, so incredibly awful
That there are no words to describe him—
And holding a great club in his hand.
And riding toward this fellow
I saw that his head was bigger   295
Than a packhorse's, or any other beast,
His hair was tufted, and his forehead
Bald and wide as two outspread
Hands, his ears all mossy,

And immense, exactly like an elephant's,   300
His eyebrows huge, his face
As if flattened. He had eyes like an owl,
A nose like a cat, and jaws
Split like a wolf's, with a boar's
Wild teeth, all yellowed, and his beard   305
Was black, his moustache crooked.
His chin met his chest, his backbone
Was long and twisted. He was leaning
On his club, his clothes as wild
As the rest of him, neither cotton nor wool   310
But the hides of two fresh-skinned bulls,
Or two oxen, that he wore hanging
From his neck, one in front, one in back.
And this creature jumped to his feet
When he saw me approaching. I had no   315
Idea if he meant to attack me,
Or what he meant to do.
I was ready to fight if I had to,
And then I saw, as he stood
All calm and still, mounted   320
On a fallen tree, that he reached up
Seventeen feet, at least.
He watched me, still as a stone,
Speaking no more than an animal,
And I thought perhaps he had   325
No brain to speak with, nor a tongue.
So I got up my courage and I said:
    "You, tell me, what are you,
Good, or evil, or what?"
    And he answered: "I am a man."   330
"What kind of man?" "The kind
You see. I'm nothing but myself."
"And what are you doing?" "I'm here,
Guarding this herd near this wood."

"Guarding them? By Saint Peter in Rome!   335
No one commands these beasts.
And how could you guard such savage
Creatures in an open field
Or a wood or anywhere else
If they're neither tied nor shut in?"   340
"I guard them so carefully, and so well,
That they'd never leave this place."
"Ridiculous! Tell me the truth!"
"Not one of them would move an inch
If he saw me coming. Whenever   345
I get my hands on one
I twist their horns so hard,
For my hands are so strong, that the others
Tremble in fear and immediately
Gather themselves around me   350
As if to cry for mercy.
But no one else could do this,
Just me. Anyone approaching
That herd would be killed at once.
And so I'm the lord of my animals.   355
And it's your turn, now, to tell me
Who you are and what you want."
    "I am, as you see, a knight,
Seeking what I cannot find:
I've hunted and I've found—nothing."   360
    "And what are you trying to find?"
    "Adventures, to test my bravery,
To prove my courage. And now
I ask you and beg you, if you can,
To counsel me, tell me—if you know one—   365
Of some adventure, some marvel."
    "As for that," he said, "too bad.
I know nothing of any 'adventures.'
No one's ever told me

Any. But just try going   370
To a certain spring, near here,
And you won't come back so easily
If you do it the way you should.
There's a path, down over there,
That will take you where you want to go.   375
Go straight ahead, if you want
To get there right away.
It's easy to get lost if you follow
All those other paths.
You'll see that spring, it surges   380
And seethes, though it's colder than marble.
It's shaded by the most beautiful tree
Nature has ever made,
With leaves forever green,
Never falling in winter.   385
And an iron bowl hangs there,
From a chain just long enough
To reach the water. And next
To the spring you'll find a stone,
You'll see for yourself—I can't   390
Describe that stone, what it's like,
For I've seen no other like it.
And then there's a chapel, a tiny
Chapel, but very beautiful.
If you'd like to sprinkle water   395
From the bowl across that stone
You'll see such a storm that no animal
Will stay in this wood—every buck,
Every doe, every stag, every boar,
And even the birds would run off,   400
Because you'd see such lightning,
Such wind, and trees splintering,
And such rain, and smashing thunder,
That if you yourself can escape

Without harm, without desperate struggling,   405
You'll have better luck than any
Knight who ever lived."
    And then I left him there,
After he'd shown me the path.
I expect it was late in the morning,   410
And getting close to noon,
When I saw the tree and the chapel.
And I can swear, and I know
It's true, that the tree was the finest
Pine anywhere in the world.   415
No rain could ever fall hard
Enough for a drop to pierce it,
But would always roll off outside.
And I saw the basin hung
From that tree, hammered of the finest   420
Gold anyone could buy.
And believe me, the spring bubbled
And boiled like steaming-hot water.
And the stone was an emerald, with holes
Bored through, just like a wineskin,   425
And under it stood four rubies,
Gleaming brighter and redder
Than the morning sun, rising
Low in the east. And this
Is what I saw, what I know: 430
Not a word I speak is untrue.
    I wanted to see the miracle
Of storm and wind and rain.
It was hardly wise, I admit it,
And as soon as I'd done it I would   435
Have taken it back, if I could,
But I took water from the bowl
And sprinkled the stone, and more
Than likely I poured too much,

For I saw the sky ripped open,   440
And lightning flashes from fourteen
Directions blinded my eyes,
And the clouds let loose sheets
Of snow and rain and hail.
The storm was so foul, so strong,   445
That a hundred times I thought
I'd be killed by bolts falling
At my feet, and by falling trees.
I was frightened half out of my wits
Till the tempest grew calm, and was gone.   450
But God gave me hope
That the storm could not last long
And soon the winds were at rest:
They dared not blow against
His will. And seeing the air   455
Clear and pure I was thrilled—
For joy, as everyone knows,
Lets sorrow soon be forgotten.
When the storm had completely vanished
I saw so many birds   460
In that pine tree (could anyone believe me?)
That it looked as if every branch,
Every twig, was hidden by birds.
And the tree was even lovelier,
For the birds all sang at once,   465
In marvellous harmony, though each
Was singing its proper song
And not a note that belonged
To one was sung by another.
And I gloried in their happiness,   470
Listening as they sang their service
Through, unhurried: I'd never
Heard joy so complete,
And no one else will hear it,

I think, unless he goes there   475
And can hear what filled me with joy
And rapture so deep that I was carried
Away—until I heard
The sound of knights approaching,
And it seemed to me there were ten: 480
But the clatter and racket were made
By a single knight, riding up.
And when I saw him, coming
Alone, I belted my saddle
Tight, and mounted. And he came   485
Angrily, riding swifter
Than an eagle, looking as fierce
As a hungry lion. And from
As far as his voice could carry
He began to hurl a challenge,   490
Crying: "You! You've done me
Harm, for no reason. You ought to
Have challenged me, were there cause for a quarrel,
Or at least demanded justice   495
Before you began to make war.
But sir! If it's in my power
This destruction you see all about you
Will fall on you. Here lies
On every hand the proof   500
Of my broken-up woods. And he
Who is injured has a right to complain.
And I do, and I'm right, for you've forced me
Out of my home with lightning
And thunder and rain. You've made   505
My life miserable and cursed be he
Who thinks that good. Here
In my wood, here in my castle,
You've launched such an attack

That no troops of soldiers, no weapons,   510
No walls could have resisted.
No one could have been safe,
Even in a fortress: not even
Hard stone walls could have helped.
Understand me! From this moment on   515
There's no truce and no peace between us!"
    At those words we rushed at each other,
Holding our shields in place,
Each covering himself. The knight
Rode a good horse, and his lance   520
Was a stout one, and I have no doubt
He sat a whole head taller
Than I did. Which was my bad luck,
For I was smaller than he was,
And his horse was stronger than mine.   525
These are things I need to say,
For they help explain my shame.
I gave him as good a blow
As I could, striking him hard,
Hitting the top of his shield,   530
And I struck so hard, with all
My strength, that my lance was shattered.
But his held together,
It was hardly light, by my faith,
But as heavy, I think, as any   535
Lance I ever saw,
Heavier and bigger than any.
And that knight struck me so stinging
A blow that it swept me backwards
And off my horse and laid me   540
Flat on the ground. And he left
Me there, shamed and exhausted,
Not bothering even to look at me.
He took my horse and left me there,

And headed back the way   545
He'd come. And I, dazed,
Just lay there, anguished, confused.
And then for a while I sat
Near the spring, and rested. How
Could I dare to follow the knight?   550
What a fool I would be! And even
Were I sure of my courage, where
Had he gone to? I had no idea.
And finally my promise came back to me:
I'd told my host I'd return   555
To his castle. I liked the idea,
And that's what I did. But walking
Was easier without my weapons
And my armor, and I left them behind,
And retraced my shameful steps.   560
When I reached his home, that night,
He treated me just as he'd done
Before, good-natured, courteous,
Exactly as I'd found him at first.
I saw nothing, neither in him   565
Nor in his daughter, that made me
Feel less welcome, nor was anything
Done to show me less honor
Than they'd shown me the previous night.
They did me great honor indeed,   570
In that house, and I thank them. And they said
No one had ever escaped,
So far as they knew, from that place
I'd gone to, without being killed
Or taken prisoner. They'd never   575
Heard a story like mine.
And so I went, and so
I returned, feeling like a fool.
And I've foolishly told you a story

I'll never tell again."   580

"By God!" said lord Yvain,
"You're my own first cousin, and we ought
To love each other, but this thing
You've hid from me, and hid for so long,
Is folly, nothing less.   585
And when I say 'folly' to you,
Please, I mean nothing offensive.
Because if I can, and if fate
Permits me, I will avenge you."
     "Ah well, it's after dinner,"   590
Said Kay, who could never be quiet.
"There are lots more words in a jug
Of wine than a barrel of beer.
They say that a cat meows
When it's full. No one moves after dinner   595
But everyone's ready to kill
A sultan and avenge all his sins!
Are your saddle-pads ready to go,
Your iron leg-armor polished,
Your banners unfurled? Quickly,   600
My lord Yvain! By God,
Are you leaving tonight or tomorrow?
Do let us know, fair sir,
Just when you begin this ordeal,
So we all can escort you. Of course,   605
All marshals and magistrates will want
To ride at your side. And I beg you,
However you arrange things, not
To leave us without proper farewells.
And if your dreams are bad tonight,   610
Perhaps you'd better stay home."

"The devil! Are you out of your mind,
Sir Kay?" said the queen. "Is there no way
To stop your wagging tongue?
Your mouth should be shamed by itself,   615
Forever dripping bile.
Plainly, your tongue dislikes you,
For it always says the worst
It knows about everyone you mention.
Cursed be any tongue   620
That can't say anything but wickedness!
It's your tongue, working as it does,
That makes everyone everywhere hate you.
It couldn't do more to betray you.
Listen: I'd charge it with treason,   625
If that tongue were mine. And anyone
Incurable ought to be tied
In front of a church, like a madman
Bound to the altar screen."
    "Indeed, my lady," said lord   630
Yvain, "I don't mind these insults.
Wherever he goes, Sir Kay
Is so talented, so wise, and so honorable
He could never be deaf or dumb.
He knows how to answer abuse   635
With good sense, and with courtesy, and he's always
Done exactly that.
You know how truly I speak.
But I've less than no interest in quarrels
Or beginning any foolishness. He   640
Who starts a fight, who strikes
The first blow, may not be the winner,
But rather he who strikes back—
And it's always better to quarrel
With a stranger than insult a friend.   645
I've no wish to act like a dog

That bristles and bares its teeth
Whenever another dog growls."

And as they spoke, the king
Came out of his room, where he'd been   650
A long time. He'd slept until
That very moment. And all
The knights, as soon as they saw him,
Jumped to their feet, but he ordered them
Back to their seats, and sat   655
Himself next to the queen,
Who told him Calgrenant's story,
Repeating it word for word,
Beautifully telling the tale
As she knew how to do. The king   660
Listened with interest, then swore
Three mighty oaths, by the soul
Of Uther Pendragon, his father,
And his son's soul, and his mother's,
That he would go to see   665
That fountain, and the storm, and all
The marvels, in two weeks time,
And swore he'd reach there on the eve
Of the Feast of Saint John the Baptist,
And there he would sleep, that night,   670
And he said he would take along
Everyone who wanted to come.
And everything the king had decided
Delighted the entire court,
For every knight and every   675
Squire was desperate to go.
But in spite of their joy and their pleasure
My lord Yvain was miserable,

For he'd meant to go alone,
And so he was sad and upset   680
At the king for planning his visit.
And what bothered him most of all
Was knowing that the right of combat
Would surely fall to Sir Kay
Rather than himself. If Kay   685
Requested it, Kay would get it—
Or even Sir Gawain, if Gawain
Chose to ask for it first.
Either of them would have it,
If either wanted it, and asked.   690
And feeling no need for their company
He decided not to wait,
But to go alone, if he could,
No matter for joy or for sorrow.
They could stay at home, if they chose,   695
But he'd made up his mind to reach
Brocelande forest in three days,
If he could, and try to find
That narrow, overgrown path—
And how anxious he was to see it!—   700
And the open fields and the castle
And all the pleasures and delights
Of that courteous young woman, well-bred
And beautiful to see, and that excellent
Knight, her father, so concerned   705
With honor, so honest and highborn,
So worthy and generous and open.
And then he would see the wild bulls
And the giant creature who guarded them.
It was hard for him to delay: 710
Such a huge creature, immense
And hideous, half-real, half-imagined,
And dark as any blacksmith.

And then he'd see, if he could,
The stone and the spring and the bowl   715
And the birds covering the pine tree,
And he'd make it rain and blow.
But he'd boast about nothing, and no one
Would know what he meant to do,
If he could help it, until   720
It was done, for honor or for shame,
And then he could let it be known.

So lord Yvain stole off,
Making sure that he met no one,
And went to his lodgings, alone.   725
His servants and attendants were there,
And he ordered his saddle put on
And spoke to his favorite squire,
One from whom he hid nothing.
    "Now listen! Come after me,   730
And bring my weapons and armor!
I'm going out through that gate,
Not on my war-horse, and only
Walking him. Be careful, and hurry;
I've a long, long way to go.   735
I want new shoes on my war-horse,
And I want him brought to me, and quickly,
And I want you to bring back the other.
But be careful, I warn you, and if anyone
Asks where I've gone, be sure   740
You tell him nothing. You may
Have counted on me before,
But never again, if you fail me."
    "My lord!" he said, "all is well.

No one will learn a thing   745
From me. Go! And I'll follow."

So lord Yvain mounted,
Meaning to avenge his cousin's
Shame before he returned,
If he could. His squire ran   750
For weapons and the war-horse, and leaped up
On its back. There was no delay,
He had plenty of horseshoes and nails.
Then he followed his master's tracks
Until he saw him, dismounted,   755
Waiting along the road,
But off to the side, in a sheltered
Spot. Armor and weapons
Were handed over, and put on,
And once he was ready Yvain   760
Wasted no time, but day
After day hurried over mountains
And across valleys and deep,
Broad forests, and strange places,
And wild places, riding   765
Through dangerous ways with many
Perils and many difficulties,
Until he reached the right road,
All choked with brambles, and dark,
And then he felt himself safe,   770
No longer able to lose
His way. Whoever might have to
Pay for it, he would not stop
Till he saw the pine shading
The fountain, and the stone, and the storm,   775
And the hail and the rain and the thunder

And wind. That night, to be sure,
He was sheltered exactly as he'd hoped,
And indeed he found his host
Still better and even more honorable   780
Than he could have expected, and as
For the girl he saw a hundred
Times more beauty and good sense
Than Calgrenant had ever spoken of,
For who can truly tell   785
The worth of a lady and a knight?
The moment a man turns toward
Goodness, nothing can sum up
His story, no tongue encompass
The honors such a knight can earn.   790
My lord Yvain slept well,
That night, and was happy, and the day
That followed showed him the wild
Bulls and the creature who guarded them,
Who showed him the path to take.   795
And yet he crossed himself
A hundred times at the sight
Of that monster, wondering how Nature
Could make such ugliness, such horror.
Then he went to the spring, and saw   800
Everything he'd wanted to see.
Not stopping for a moment, standing
Erect, he poured the bowl
Of water directly on the stone,
And at once it blew and it rained   805
And created the storm he'd been told of.
And when God brought back fair weather
The birds came to the pine tree
And sang their wonderfully joyous
Songs above that dangerous   810
Spring. But before their rapture

Ended, the knight appeared,
Blazing with anger and pounding
On the ground as if he were hunting
A stag. And they rushed at each other,   815
Fighting furiously, as if
To show how they hated, and would kill.
They each swung mighty lances,
And slashed and smashed away
Until both their shields were cracked,   820
And their shoulder mail was broken,
And their spears were split and splintered,
With pieces flying in the air.
Then they drew their swords and came forward,
And the slicing of their swords cut through   825
The straps holding up their shields,
And the shields themselves were hacked
To bits, from top to bottom,
So the shreds hung down and neither
Covered their bodies nor defended them,   830
So split and torn that their gleaming
Swords hit directly
On each other's sides
And arms and hips. They went
At each other savagely, desperately,   835
Neither moving from his spot
Any more than a block of stone.
There were never two knights angrier
Or more determined to kill or be killed.
And they chose their blows with care,   840
Struggling to make them work.
Their helmets began to cave in,
And break, and the metal in their mail-shirts
Began to snap, and blood
Began to flow, the mail   845
Growing so hot it protected

Their bodies no more than a cloak.
Stabbing at each other's faces
It was wonderful that so fierce and hard
A fight could go on for so long,   850
But both were knights of such heart
And such courage that neither would ever
Yield a foot of ground
Until mortally wounded. And both
Were as noble as brave, for neither   855
Attempted to wound the other's
Horse, neither wishing
To stoop so low. They sat
In their saddles the whole time, never
Setting a foot on the ground.   860
What a beautiful fight it was!
And at last lord Yvain
Shattered the other's helmet
With a blow that stunned him, left him dizzy
And weak and frightened, for no one   865
Had ever dealt him such a terrible
Stroke. Under his cracked
Helmet his head was split
To the brain, and blood poured
From his skull and stained his gleaming   870
Mail-shirt, and he felt such crushing
Pain that his courage failed him.
And indeed his heart did him
No injustice, for he felt himself fatally
Wounded and that nothing could save him.   875
And as fast as he could think, he turned
And galloped straight toward his castle,
Where the drawbridge was lowered and the gate
Swung wide and open, with lord
Yvain galloping after him,   880
Spurring his horse to its fastest.

Like a falcon swooping on its prey
When he sees it run, and almost
Snatching it up, close
But missing, so Yvain pursued him,   885
Almost able to grasp him,
But just unable to reach
Though so close behind he could hear
The knight groaning in pain,
Closer and closer, but unable   890
To catch him. And he rode still faster,
All his effort lost
If he can't get him, alive
Or dead, for he remembered the taunts
And insults spoken by Sir Kay.   895
Nor had he fulfilled the promise
Made to his cousin, and no one
Would ever believe him without
Some true tokens of victory.
Their galloping chase came straight   900
To the castle gate, and both
Rode right in, but neither
Man nor woman walked
In those streets, as they galloped down them,
Both of them riding swiftly   905
Right to the palace door.

Now that door was high and broad,
But the entry was exceedingly narrow,
So neither two men nor two horses
Could go through at once unless   910
They were crushed uncomfortably against
One another, and directly in the center,
For it was built exactly like a trap

Set for a rat when he comes
Hunting what was never his.   915
And a sharp blade hung
Up above, which shot viciously
Down on its tracks when anything
Touched its trigger, or even
Came close, no matter how gently.   920
And just below the door
Were two hidden springs, connected
To a sliding iron grate
That could cut like a knife. If anyone
Stepped onto this device   925
The grate came sliding down
And whoever was caught beneath it
Was crushed, was cut to pieces.
And just in the middle the path
Narrowed so sharply that it might   930
Have been a track through the woods.
And knowing his way, the beaten
Knight rushed through this passage,
With lord Yvain dashing
So closely behind him, galloping   935
So fast that he reached out his hand
And pulled at the bow of his saddle.
And it was lucky he leaned so far forward,
Stretching to grasp at his enemy,
For without that bit of luck   940
The grate and the knife would have chopped him
In two, for his horse tripped
The trigger, thundering across
The beams, and like a devil out of hell
The gate came crashing down,   945
Striking the saddle and the horse's
Hindquarters and slicing them through.
But lord Yvain, with God's

Great grace, was barely touched,
For the blade came level with his back,   950
Cutting off both his spurs
Just even with his heels. And as
He tumbled, terrified, to the ground,
The defeated knight with his mortal
Wound escaped him. There stood   955
Another gate, just beyond
The one where they'd been, and the knight
He'd been chasing rode straight on through
And it shut behind him, and so
He made his escape. And there   960
My lord Yvain was caught,
Tormented and at a loss,
Finding himself in this closed
Passageway, covered with a gilded
Ceiling, its walls decorated   965
With beautiful, expensive paints.
But nothing pained him so much
As not knowing just where the knight
He'd been chasing had vanished.
He stood uncertain, and then   970
A small door opened
In a small room close by,
And a girl came out, alone,
Beautiful and well-mannered, and then
She shut the door behind her.   975
And seeing lord Yvain
At first she was deeply distressed.
    "Knight!" she exclaimed. "You've surely
Come in an evil hour.
If anyone sees you here   980
They'll cut you into tiny pieces,
For the lord of this castle is mortally
Wounded, and of course I know

You've killed him. My lady's grief
Is so powerful, and everyone around her   985
Weeps so violently they're almost
Ready to die of it, if they knew
You were here! But their grief is so great
That once they knew where you were
They'd kill you, or capture you, as it pleased them,   990
And nothing could stop them if they came
To attack you." And lord Yvain
Answered her: "And yet, if God
So wills it, they'll neither kill me
Nor have me in their hands." "No,"   995
She said, "for I shall do everything
I can to assist you. It's better
For a knight not to be afraid.
And I know you for a noble knight,
Seeing how little you're frightened.   1000
Understand me: I would do you honor,
I would serve you, if I could, as you
Have already done for me.
My lady once sent me to Arthur's
Court with a message, and I suppose   1005
I was neither as wise nor as courteous
Nor in anything what I ought to have been
As a girl at the king's high court.
And none of the knights would stoop
To exchange a word with me,   1010
Except you, who stand here now,
But you, out of kindness and mercy,
Were courteous and helped me. And for the honor
You did me then I offer you,
In exchange, this reward. I know   1015
There is nothing you've asked. I know.
But I knew you as soon as I saw you,
You're the son of King Urien, and your name

Is lord Yvain. And you
Can be certain, you can be sure,   1020
That trusting my words, you'll never
Be captured or hurt. Accept
This little ring, and if
You please return it to me
When it's done its work, and you're free."   1025
Then she gave him the little ring
And told him it had such power
That, just as bark hid the wood
Of a tree, and no one could see it,
So this ring would conceal anyone   1030
Who wore it, as long as the stone
Sat in his palm: there was nothing
To fear from anyone if he wore it
As she'd said, for no one could possibly
See him, no matter how keen   1035
Their eyes, any more than they saw
Through bark to the wood underneath.
And lord Yvain was happy.
And when she'd told him these things
She led him to a couch covered   1040
With cloth so rich that the Duke
Of Austria could never afford it,
And sat him there, and said
If he cared to eat she would fetch him
Food. And he said he would.   1045
And running into her room
The girl returned, as fast
As possible, with a roasted fowl
And a cake and a tablecloth
And a full jug of wine   1050
Made from good grapes, and a white
Goblet covering it, and invited him
To dine. And needing that food

He ate it gladly and with good will.

And when he had eaten and drunk   1055
Knights were hurrying through
The castle, hunting him,
For their lord, already lying
On his bier, wanted revenge.
And she said to him: "Friend!   1060
Do you hear? Everyone's hunting you.
What a lot of noise they're making!
But no matter who comes or goes
Don't let their noise make you move,
For there's no way they'll ever find you   1065
If you never move from this couch.
Oh, this room will be full of men
At arms, angry, fierce,
Just wanting to find you out,
And I suspect they'll bring the body   1070
In here, getting it ready
For burial, and they'll crawl under benches
And beds, seeking you. And you,
A man who feels no fear,
Ought to find it amusing,   1075
Seeing so many men
So blind, so desperate and defeated,
And all the time so deluded,
That they'll be half mad with rage.
I know nothing more to tell you,   1080
And I cannot stay here any longer.
But I'm grateful to almighty God
Who's given me this chance
To do something that might please you:

It's something I'd wanted to do."   1085
    And then she went on her way,
And after she'd turned and gone out
Everyone else swarmed by,
Rushing to the gates from both sides,
Armed with clubs and swords,   1090
A huge crowd pushing
And shoving, furious, savage.
And then they saw in front
Of the gate the horse cut in half.
And then they thought it was certain   1095
That once the gates were opened
They'd find him in there, the man
They wanted to kill. So they had
Those gates drawn up, those gates
That had killed so many men,   1100
And of course they set no trap
Nor primed the springs, but rushed
Across in a tumbling mob.
And they found the other half
Of the horse, dead, lying   1105
On the threshold, but none of them had eyes
Keen enough to see
Lord Yvain, though they'd cheerfully have killed him.
And he watched their fury, as they stormed
And screamed and ranted and roared.   1110
And they cried: "This is impossible!
There's no window here, no door,
That anything could get through, except
A bird, which can fly, or a squirrel,
Or perhaps a woodchuck or a rat   1115
Or something as small or smaller,
For the windows are barred, and the gates
Were all of them shut, as soon
As our lord came through. His body

Has got to be here, dead   1120
Or alive, for there's nothing out there.
There's more than half the saddle
Out there, we see that, all right,
But there's nothing to be seen of him
Except his cut-off spurs,   1125
Sheared away from his feet.
Now! Let's hunt him in every
Corner, and stop all this blather,
For he's got to be here, he's got to,
Unless we're all bewitched   1130
Or the demons of hell have taken him."
    And so they all of them, wild
With rage, hunted him all over
The room, beating on everything—
Walls and couches and chairs—   1135
But their blows never touched the couch
Where Yvain lay resting, so nothing
Hurt him. But they banged and smashed
About so furiously, bashing
Everywhere, fighting immense   1140
Battles like blind men in the dark,
Pounding as blind men pound
When they hunt what they cannot see—
And then, suddenly, as they searched
And searched again, under beds,   1145
Under stools, there appeared a woman
As lovely as any creature on earth.
No one had spoken a word
Of so splendid a lady, and yet
Her grief was so intense   1150
She seemed ready to take her own life.
And then she cried out so loudly
That she seemed to have exhausted herself
And dropped to the ground, unconscious.

And when they lifted her up   1155
She began to tear at her clothes
Like a woman gone mad, and she pulled
At her hair, and ripped it out,
And she tore at her dress, and at every
Step fell in a faint,   1160
And nothing could relieve her pain,
For she saw her lord carried
In and laid on his death bed,
And all her happiness was ended,
And so she cried and wailed.   1165
Holy water and the cross
And uplifted candles were carried
In front, by the nuns from a convent,
And then came the Holy Word
And incense and priests, the stewards   1170
Of eternal absolution, which miserable
Souls are always seeking.

And lord Yvain listened
To that weeping beyond description,
Which no words can describe, which never   1175
Can be written in a book. And the solemn
Procession went by, but then
In the middle of the room a crowd
Milled around the bier,
For fresh red blood began   1180
To run from the corpse's cold wounds,
And this was positive proof
That whoever had fought their lord
In battle, and beaten him, and killed him,
Was surely still there. And everyone   1185
Hunted and searched again,

And ransacked the room, and turned it
Upside down, till they all
Were sweating in confusion and pain,
And all of it caused by that blood   1190
Trickling down in plain sight.
And this time blow after blow
Fell on my lord Yvain,
Where he lay, but he never moved.
And the crowd grew wilder and wilder   1195
As the wounds stayed open, and bled,
For no one knew why they bled
Or who was responsible. And this one
Said to that one, and babbled:
    "The murderer is here, he's here,   1200
And no one can see him, no one.
This is a wonder, it is witchery."
And such pain and sorrow afflicted
The lady that she left her senses
And shrieked like a mad wild creature: 1205
    "God! God! Can't they find
The murderer, the traitor, who killed
My dear sweet lord? Good?
Oh, he was better than good!
It will be Your fault, it will,   1210
My God, if You let him escape.
I accuse no one but You
For stealing him out of our sight.
No one has ever known
Such violence, and such wrong, as You do me,   1215
Not even allowing me to see
This man, who must be so near.
And surely, seeing nothing,
I claim that some phantom, some demon,
Has placed himself between us,   1220
And I am completely bewitched.

Or he is a coward, and afraid.
What a coward he must be, to fear
My tears, a coward of cowards
Not to dare show me his face!   1225
Ah demon, cowardly creature,
Why tremble and shake at the sight
Of me? You were brave with my lord!
Cheating, empty thing,
If I only had you in my power!   1230
Let me lay my hands on you!
And how could a creature like you
Ever kill my lord, except
By treachery and tricks? My lord
Could never be beaten by you,   1235
No, not if he saw your face.
For neither God nor man
Ever knew any man like him,
And no one like him is left.
Had you been merely mortal   1240
You'd never have dared oppose him,
For there was no one like him, no one."

And so the lady struggled,
Fighting with everything, and herself,
And so she tormented and tore   1245
At herself. And they all renewed
Her grief, which couldn't have been greater,
Until the body was borne off for burial.
And after beating about, and hunting,
And shouting, her people were so tired   1250
That they'd given up, in weariness,
Finding no one they could see, no one
They could blame. And all the nuns

And priests finished their service
And left, some returning   1255
To their church, some praying
At their lord's new tomb. —But the girl
In her room had no interest in any
Of this, her thoughts were only
Of lord Yvain, and coming   1260
To him as quickly as she could
She said: "Good sir! These people
Have been hunting you in crowds. They've raised
An enormous racket in here,
Beating about in every   1265
Corner with more zeal than hounds
Barking after partridge or quail.
You must have been afraid."
    "By God!" he said. "You're right!
I never expected such fear.   1270
And still, if possible, I'd like
To watch through some crack in a wall
Or some window, and see the funeral
Procession, and the corpse." And yet
He was interested neither in funeral   1275
Nor corpse; he'd gladly have watched
As both of them burned, if it cost him
A thousand marks. A thousand?
More likely three thousand, by God!
It was the lady of that castle he wanted   1280
To see, it was she he spoke of.
And the girl put him in front of
A tiny window, repaying him
As well as she could the honor
He had once done her. And from   1285
That window my lord Yvain
Could watch the beautiful lady,
Who said: "Good sir! May God

Surely have mercy on your soul,
For never have I known of a knight   1290
Anywhere who was your equal,
In anything as worthy as you!
Your honor, my beloved good lord,
Was never equalled by any
Knight, nor your courtesy. Kindness   1295
And openness were your friends, and courage
And bravery rode at your side.
May your soul join the company
Of saints, my good sweet lord!"
Then she beat at herself, and tore   1300
At everything her hands could reach.
And lord Yvain suffered
Such pain, it was hard, no matter
What happened, to keep from running
To grasp her hands. But the girl   1305
Begged him, and counselled him, and scolded him,
Though always gracefully and in good taste,
To keep from foolish things,
And she said: "You're well off right here.
Let nothing take you away   1310
Until this sorrow has eased
And all these people have gone,
As soon they must. Behave
As I urge, exactly as I
Urge you to do, and many   1315
Good things may come to you.
And the best thing will be to stay
Where you are and watch these people,
Inside and out, going
Their ways, and none of them seeing   1320
You, and everything for the best.
But guard your tongue, keep it
In control, for violence and passion   1322a

And impulse only cause trouble,   1322b
If you give them the chance, and I call that   1322c
Wicked and cowardly, not brave.   1322d
Be careful, if you think of being
A fool, to do nothing at all.
The wise man hides his folly   1325
And lets the good go to work,
If he can. Behave like the wise,
Who keep their heads out of danger—
They'd take no ransom for that head
Of yours! Be careful of yourself,   1330
And remember my advice! Be calm
And wait for my return,
For I dare not stay here longer.
If I stay on here with you
Perhaps they'll begin to suspect me,   1335
Not seeing me there with the others,
Milling in that crowd down there,
And I might be severely punished."

So off she goes, and he stays,
Not knowing what he ought to do.   1340
He sees them about to bury
The corpse, and he's had no chance
To snatch some trophy for himself,
Something to prove beyond doubt
That he'd conquered and killed the man.   1345
Without some evidence, some proof,
He might be utterly disgraced.
For Kay is so savage, so spiteful,
So full of insults, so mean,
He could never hold him off,   1350
And Kay would go on, forever

Sniping and insulting, exactly
As he'd done the other day.
Those taunts had never left
His heart, still beat there, fresh,   1355
And yet a new love had softened
That rancor with its sugar and honey,
A love that had hunted in his heart
And completely conquered its prey.
His enemy had captured his heart,   1360
He loved the creature who hated
Him most. Not suspecting a thing,
The lady had avenged her lord's death.
She'd managed a greater vengeance
Than anything she could have accomplished   1365
By herself, without Love's assistance,
Who came to him so gently
That it struck his heart through his eyes.
And this is a longer-lasting
Wound than a sword or a spear   1370
Can inflict, for a sword-blow is healed
And well once a doctor has cared for it,
And the wounds of Love grow worse
The nearer they are to their cure.
And thus lord Yvain is wounded   1375
And can never again be cured,
For Love itself has conquered him.
Places she has always avoided
Are places Love sometimes seeks;
She longs for no lodging, no landlord,   1380
But this one, and the proof is that nothing
Can be bad, or too low, so long
As Love finds herself there.
Everywhere else is empty,
She searches so hard. How shameful   1385
For Love to act this way,

Picking the worst of all places,
The lowest, the most base, as readily
As the best, though this time she's chosen
The best of all possible homes.   1390
Love is most welcome, here,
And here she'll be shown great honor,
And here she'd do well to stay.
And so Love should, a creature
Of such nobility that it seems   1395
Incredible she could dare descend
To shameful, vulgar places.
Like someone who carefully spreads
Balm on cinders and ashes,
Who hates honor and cherishes   1400
Shame, who mixes sugar
And bile, and honey and fat.
But this time Love was different,
Choosing a highborn home
For which no one could possibly scold her.   1405
    And now the dead knight was buried,
And the crowds of his people were gone,
No priests, no knights, no soldiers,
No ladies remained, only
That lady who continued to grieve.   1410
She stayed alone, often
Clutching at her throat, wringing
Her hands, beating her palms,
Reading psalms from a prayerbook
Illumined in letters of gold.   1415
And lord Yvain still stands
At the window, watching her, staring,
And the more he watches the more
He loves her and the more she charms him.
She wept and she read, but he wished   1420
She would give them up, and turn

To him, and give him leave to speak.
Love had caught him at the window
And put this desire in his heart.
But his desire is foolish, and he knows it: 1425
How could he believe, how
Could he trust it to happen? And he says:
"What a fool I am, to want
What I'll never have. Her lord
Is dead of his wounds, and can I   1430
Believe in peace between us?
By God, I understand nothing!
She loathes me, now, and not
For nothing, and not wrongly.
But 'now' is the crucial word,   1435
For a woman's mind has a thousand
Directions. And perhaps that 'now'
Will change. Oh, surely it will change,
And how stupid of me to stand here
Lost in despair. God grant   1440
That she changes soon! For Love
Has decided to put me forever
In her power, and Love takes what it wants!
Not to accept Love's wish
When Love comes, and Love asks, is more   1445
Than wicked, it is treachery. And I say,
And whoever worships Love
Let him listen, that a deserter from Love
Deserves no happiness. I may lose,
But I'll always love my enemy.   1450
How could I ever hate her,
If I wish to be loyal to Love?
What Love wants, I want. But she,
Should she accept me as a lover?
She should, for it is she I love.   1455
I call her my enemy: she hates me,

And she has reason to hate me, remembering
How I killed the man she loved.
And I, am I her enemy?
Never, but only her lover,   1460
For who have I loved like this?
I feel pain, seeing her beautiful
Hair, finer than gold,
And gleaming. Pain and anger
Fill me, when she twists and breaks   1465
That hair. I know nothing can dry
The tears falling from her eyes.
And all of it makes me miserable.
Her eyes are forever full
Of tears, tears without end,   1470
And yet no eyes were ever
Lovelier. I weep because
She weeps, but my greatest pain
Is seeing how she wounds her face,
Though it can't deserve it. I've never   1475
Beheld such a perfect face,
So glowing and intense, so vividly
Colored. And how it afflicts me
To see her clutching at her throat!
Surely, she cannot help   1480
Herself, she does the worst
She can. And yet no crystal,
No mirror, is as clear or as smooth.
Lord! Why is she so
Obsessed, why can't she hurt herself   1485
Less? Why wring those beautiful
Hands, and beat and scratch
At her breast? How wonderfully fine
To see her, in some happy mood,
If her beauty shines in such anger!   1490
Oh yes, I can swear to that:

Never before has Nature
So outdone herself in beauty,
For here all boundaries are exceeded.
And how could it possibly have happened?   1495
How could such beauty exist?
Where could such beauty have come from?
God must have made her Himself,
With His own bare hands, to make Nature
Gape. And it's all used up,   1500
Nature could not make another,
She'd only be wasting her time.
God Himself, if He wanted
To try, could not do it again,
No matter how hard He tried,   1505
For it could not be done, not ever."

And so my lord Yvain
Thought of that lady, tortured
With grief. And when will it happen
Again that a man held   1510
In prison as Yvain was held,
Knowing his life in danger,
Will love so madly that he'll never
Beg for himself, when no one
Else could be begging for him?   1515
He stayed standing at the window
Till he saw the lady leave
And both drawbridges were lowered
Back into place. Some other
Knight might have been miserable,   1520
Preferring freedom, wishing
To remain no longer where he was,
But to him it was all the same

If they shut the gates or opened them.
Indeed, if they left them open   1525
There could be no question of leaving,
Not even were the lady to grant him
Permission to go, gladly
Pardoning him for the death of her lord,
Freeing him in safety. Because   1530
It was Love, and it was Shame, that held him,
Standing to his right and his left.
He was shamed if he went away,
For no one would believe he'd done
What he'd done, and seen what he'd seen.   1535
And then he felt so strong
A desire at least to see
The lady, if nothing more,
That prison meant nothing. He would rather
Die than leave. —And now   1540
The girl returned, wanting
To keep him company, to amuse
And entertain him, and more
Than ready to bring him anything
His heart desired. But love,   1545
Seizing him, left him thoughtful,
Distracted, languid and weak.
And she said: "My lord Yvain!
What sort of day have you had?"
"The sort that pleases me immensely."   1550
"Pleases you? By God! Are you telling
The truth? What? How
Can you be amused, seeing
Them hunting and intending to kill you?"
"Surely, good friend," he said,   1555
"I've no interest at all in dying,
And yet, as God is my witness,
I've delighted in everything I've seen,

I'm pleased and will always be pleased."
"We can leave that subject alone,"   1560
She said, "for I see quite well
What those words are meant to mean.
I'm neither so simple or dull
That I can't understand such talk.
But follow me, for I need   1565
To find some quick and easy
Way to free you from your prison.
Please God, I'll have you free
Tonight or tomorrow. Come,
I'll show you the way." And he answered: 1570
"One thing is certain: I'll never
Leave like a thief, I'll never
Sneak away in the dark.
And when all your people are gathered
Out in those streets, I can leave   1575
With far more honor than if
I went by night." And after
These words they entered her little
Room. And the girl, who knew
What she was doing, was anxious to bring him   1580
Whatever he wanted, freely
Supplying all he needed,
As she'd promised to do. And when
There was time, she turned in her mind
Exactly what he'd said, and how pleased   1585
He had been with everything he saw,
Even as they'd hunted him in the room
And tried to kill him, and longed to.

And this girl stood so high in her lady's

Favor there was nothing she feared   1590
To say, whatever her words
Might lead to. The lady told her
Everything, and she kept things to herself.
Then why be afraid to offer
Her mistress consolation, and advice   1595
That would bring her honor? The first time
The two were alone she said:
"Lady! I find myself
Astonished at this wildness and violence.
My lady! Do you think this sort   1600
Of sorrow will bring back your lord?"
"No," she answered, "but I'd rather
Be dead of my grief." "And why?"
"To go where he has gone."
"Follow him? May God protect you   1605
And find you another lord
As good, as He can do."
"You've never spoken so huge
A lie, there is no one as good."
"There are better, and if you would accept him   1610
I'd bring him here, in proof."
"Leave me! Be quiet! I will never
Find one." "My lady, you will,
If you'll only permit it. Tell me,
If you please, who will defend   1615
Your lands when King Arthur comes,
And he comes in another week,
Seeking the stone and the fountain?
Our Lady Sauvage has long since
Sent word of his coming, sent a letter   1620
With that news. Ah! How truly
She has sought to help you! What you need
To be planning is how to defend
Your fountain, and with whose help,

And all you can do is weep!   1625
My lady, dear lady, delay
No longer. I beg you! None
Of your knights is worth as much
As a single chambermaid, none of them,
And you know it, lady. The best   1630
Of your knights can barely lift
A shield or pick up a spear.
You have plenty of weak-kneed men,
But none of them have the courage
To mount a war-horse and sit tall.   1635
And the king is coming with so huge
An army that nothing will stop him."
The lady knew very well
That this was honest advice,
But she had her foolish side,   1640
Like almost every woman
Alive, totally blind
To her madness, excusing herself
As she pushed away what she really
Wanted. "Leave me!" she cried,   1645
"Not another word! And run
For your life if you speak like this
Again! You talk too much,
You tire me." "Surely, my lady!
How easy to see you're a woman,   1650
For women grow angry when anyone
Gives them good advice."

She left, and the lady was alone,
And when she'd thought a bit more
She knew she'd been very wrong.   1655
And all her desire was to know

How the girl could have proven
That a better knight could be found
Than her lord had ever been.
And she wished she could hear her explain,   1660
But she'd forbidden the girl to speak.
So, longing to hear, she waited
For the girl to return. But nothing
She'd said had made any difference:
The girl began at once: 1665
"Oh, my lady! Is it fitting
To kill yourself with grief?
By God! Get control of yourself,
Stop it, if only for shame.
No highborn lady ought   1670
To keep up her mourning so long.
Remember your honor, think
Of your high and noble birth.
Do you think that all the honor
On earth died with your lord?   1675
A hundred as good, or better,
Have been left in this world." "May the good Lord
Destroy me, but you lie in your teeth!
How could you show me a single
Man with a name as noble   1680
As my lord enjoyed all his life?"
"You wouldn't be grateful, if I did,
I know you wouldn't. You'd fly
In a fury, there'd be insults, there'd be threats."
"Not at all, I assure you I won't."   1685
"How good it would be, how lucky,
My lady, for you and your future,
If you let it please you—and may God
Give you the will to be pleased!
And why should I hold my tongue?   1690
No one listens to the likes

Of us. You'll think me presumptuous,
But I'll tell you exactly what I think.
When a pair of knights have come
Together in battle, and one   1695
Has beaten the other, who seems
To you most worthy? Me,
I give the prize to the victor.
And how does it seem to you?"
"I think you're trying to trick me,   1700
Trying to trap me with my words."
"Good lord! Well, you
Can be sure I'm right, I know
What I'm saying. I can prove it, too.
The knight who defeated your lord   1705
Was better than he was. He beat him,
And then he chased him bravely
Here to his home, and then
He locked him up in his house."
"Oh now," she answered, "I hear   1710
The worst nonsense in the world.
Enough! You've a wicked heart.
Enough! You're a stupid, tiresome
Girl. Enough of your silliness!
Never come in my presence   1715
With praise for that man. Enough!"
"Indeed, my lady! As I told you,
I knew you'd be ungrateful.
I told you I knew. But you gave me
Your word, you promised, that if   1720
I spoke you'd listen and not
Be angry. You haven't kept
Your promise, you gave me your word
And you broke it. I spoke because
You wished it, you asked me to speak,   1725
But you're angry, and I've lost by my words."

And then she returned to the room
Where she kept my lord Yvain
Resting and waiting in great comfort,
But nothing pleased him, when he heard   1730
He could not see the lady,
And though she repeated her quarrel
With her mistress, he paid no attention.
And the lady, too, lay awake
All night, at war with herself,   1735
Terribly worried how
To protect her wonderful spring,
And beginning to regret how she'd scolded
And insulted her servant, and shown her
Such violent contempt, for she was sure,   1740
Completely certain, that it was not
For a bribe or any reward,
Nor because she loved him, that the girl
Had begun to speak of her husband's
Killer; she knew she loved her   1745
Better than him, and her advice
Intended no shame and no harm:
The girl was too loyal a friend.
And like that! the lady suddenly
Changed toward the girl she'd abused,   1750
Worried, now, that she'd never
Ever love her again.
And he whom she'd pushed away
She calmly excused, convinced
By reason and by argument that nothing   1755
He'd done had injured her.
And so she debated with herself,
As if he were standing in front of her.

And these were the words of her argument:
"Now," she said, "could you possibly   1760
Deny that you killed my lord?"
"That," he replied, "I could never
Say. I admit it." "Then tell me,
Did you do it because you hate me,
To hurt me, to make me miserable?"   1765
"May death take me here
And now if I ever meant you
Harm." "Then you've done me no wrong,
And you've done no wrong to him:
He'd have killed you, if he could.   1770
And thus it seems to me
I've judged correctly, and well."
And so, by this same proof,
She found reason and right and wisdom,
And no need for her to hate him,   1775
Ensuring herself what she wanted
And all the time igniting
Herself, like smoking wood,
Bursting into flame when it's stirred,
Smouldering if no one blows it   1780
Awake. If the girl had come to her
Now, she'd have won the argument
She'd tried so hard to win
And been so insulted for beginning.
And in the morning she came   1785
And began it all over again,
Starting where she'd stopped before.
And it made the lady lower
Her head, for she knew she'd done wrong
To be angry and insult her as she'd done.   1790
And now she wanted to make
Amends, and asked the knight's name,
And his birth, and what he was like,

And wisely humbling herself.
And she said: "I beg your pardon   1795
For my offensive words, and my swollen
Pride, speaking to you
Like a fool. I will follow your advice.
But tell me, if you know, what sort
Of man is this knight of whom   1800
You've told me so much, arguing
His cause, and what was his birth?
And if he's worthy of me,
And he wishes to do it, I'll marry him,
I promise you, I'll make him lord   1805
Of my lands and of me. But he'll have
To manage it all so there'll be
No gossip, so no one will say,
'Ah, that's the one, the woman
Who married her husband's murderer'."   1810
"In the name of God, my lady,
So let it be. Your lord
Will be the noblest, most honorable,
The handsomest of Abel's lineage."
"And his name?" "My lord Yvain."   1815
"Indeed! Not badly born
At all, but of great good birth,
I know—the son of King Urien."
"Exactly, my lady! You're right."
"And when are we to see him?"   1820
"In five days' time." "Too long.
I wish he were already here.
Let him come tonight, or at least
Tomorrow." "My lady! No one
Could come so far in one day.   1825
But I'll send one of my servant
Boys, who can run very fast,
And I think he can get to King Arthur's

Court by tomorrow night,
At least. And Arthur's court   1830
Is where we must seek him." "That's more
Than long enough. Those
Will be long, long days. But tell him
He must be back tomorrow
Night, and be faster than usual.   1835
Tell him, if he does his best,
He can turn two days into one.
And tonight there'll be a moon,
So he can turn the night into day.
And tell him once he comes back   1840
I'll give him whatever he wants."
"Let all these problems be mine:
I'll have him here in your hands
In three days at the latest.
And meanwhile send for your soldiers,   1845
To ask their advice about
The king, who's surely coming.
To keep up the custom of defending
Your spring, you need to consult
With them, to seek their counsel.   1850
But none of them are likely
To boast about coming. Or come.
And then you'll be able to say
With justice that you had to marry.
A famous knight begs   1855
For your hand, but you dare not accept him
If a single objection is heard.
And I'll tell you exactly their answer:
I know they're all so worthless
That to get the burden on someone   1860
Else's back, not theirs,
They'll all be falling at your feet
And thanking you over and over

For getting them out of their trouble.
Whoever's afraid of his shadow   1865
Will gladly avoid, if he can,
Any meeting with a spear or a javelin.
Cowards don't like those games."
And the lady answered: "By God,
I'll do it, I give you my word!   1870
And besides, I'd already thought
Of exactly the plan you describe,
And that's exactly what we'll do.
But why are you waiting here?
Go! Don't waste a minute,   1875
Arrange what you have to arrange.
And I shall stay with my people."
And so they ended their talk.
And the girl pretended to hunt
For my lord Yvain in his own   1880
Country, while every day
She saw to his bath and his grooming.
And more: she had him dressed
In fine red wool, lined
With gleaming new fur. She leaves out   1885
Nothing he needs to properly
Adorn himself, she lends him
Everything: a golden necklace,
Set with precious stones,
The sort that make men graceful,   1890
And a belt, and a purse to hang from it,
Woven of gold brocade.
And so she dressed him perfectly,
And assured her mistress that the servants
She'd sent had all returned,   1895
And all had served them well.
"What?" she demanded. "Is he here,
My lord Yvain?" "He is."

"He's here? Then let him come to me,
In secret and without any noise,   1900
While no one is here in my room.
Be sure that no one else
Gets in, for I'd hate to have
A fourth." So the girl left her,
And went where her guest was waiting,   1905
Never showing in her face
The happiness she felt in her heart.
And she told him the lady knew everything,
And how she had hidden him away,
And she said: "My lord Yvain!   1910
By God, there's nothing left
To hide. It's all come out,
My lady knows it all,
Who's furious with me, and hates me,
And can't stop her scolding and reproaching.   1915
But this much assurance she's given me:
I can bring you to her and no one
Will stop us, and no one will harm you.
This shouldn't displease you, I think,
Except—and I'll tell you no lies,   1920
For that would be disloyal—
She wants you to be her prisoner,
She wishes to have your body
For herself, not even your heart
To be free." "Surely," he answered,   1925
"I agree, I've no objections.
I want to be her prisoner."
"And so you'll be, by this hand
I lay on your shoulder! Now come
And do as I say, behave   1930
So humbly when you're in her presence
That your jailing won't be too bad.
And don't be too concerned!

I suspect your confinement won't be
A burden, or bother you much."   1935
And so she led him off,
Worrying him a bit, then making him
Calmer, and giving him hints
Of the prison he was going into.
What lover escapes his prison?   1940
She was right, calling it a prison:
Whoever's in love is in jail.

And so she led my lord
Yvain by the hand, and took him
There where he'd be dearly cherished,   1945
But believing he'd never be welcomed.
No wonder he believed every word.
And they found the lady seated
On a soft red cushion. And I promise
You this: my lord Yvain   1950
Was mightily afraid, entering
That room, and finding the lady,
Who spoke not a single word.
And that made him more afraid,
Half overcome with fear   1955
And believing himself betrayed.
And he stood there so long, motionless,
That finally the girl spoke up,
Saying: "A thousand curses
On her head, who brings a knight   1960
To a beautiful lady's room,
And he won't go near her, or speak,
Too stupid to tell her his name."
And then she took him by the arm

And told him: "Come here, knight!   1965
And don't be afraid of my lady,
She's not about to kill you.
Try to appease her, make peace.
I'll join you. Pray for her pardon
For killing Esclados the Red,   1970
The knight who was her husband."
And lord Yvain clasped
His hands, and fell to his knees,
And spoke like a true lover:
"Lady! Rather than beg   1975
For your mercy I'll thank you for anything
You wish to do with me.
Nothing you do could displease me."
"Really? And what if I kill you?"
"Lady! Your will be done.   1980
You'll never hear me complain."
"I've never heard such a thing,"
She said, "that you put yourself
Completely in my power, and no one
Compels you." "Lady! Truly,   1985
No power on earth could be
As strong as this which orders
Me to consent to your will,
Completely and in every regard.
Nothing could make me hesitate   1990
To do whatever you wish.
And if I could atone
For that death, in which I did nothing
Wrong, I'd do it at once."
"What?" she said, "Now tell me   1995
If you ought to be forgiven,
If you truly did no wrong
When you killed my own true lord?"
"Lady!" he answered, "pardon me,

When your lord attacked me, and he did,   2000
Why was I wrong to defend
Myself? When you kill a man
And defend yourself against death,
Tell me what harm has been done?"
"None, if you look at it right.   2005
And it seems to me that nothing
Would be gained by having you killed.
But tell me, I'd like to know,
From where you gather this strength
That orders you to consent,   2010
Without contradiction, to whatever
I wish. I grant you your pardon.
Come, be seated, and tell me
How you come to be vanquished."
"Lady! That power comes   2015
From my heart, which bends toward you.
My desire comes from my heart."
"Sweet friend, what drove your heart?"
"Oh lady, my eyes!" "And your eyes?"
"The beauty I see in you."   2020
"But what has beauty done wrong?"
"Lady! It has made me love."
"Love? And whom?" "You,
Dear lady." "Me?" "Indeed."
"Really? And how?" "So nothing   2025
Could be greater, so my heart wishes
To be near you and can only be found
With you, so I think of nothing
Else, so I surrender completely
To you, so I love you more   2030
Than myself, so I'm ready to live
Or die, exactly as you choose."
"And would you dare to defend
My spring, defend it for me?"

"Oh lady, against the world!"   2035
"Then know: we have come together."
    They'd agreed, and it didn't take long!
And the lady, who had already spoken
To her barons and all her men,
Said: "From here we shall go   2040
To the hall where my soldiers are gathered,
Who all have advised and counselled
That because of the need we all see
I ought to marry again.
And because of that need I will.   2045
I give myself to you.
I cannot refuse so good
A knight, the son of a king."

And so the girl has done
Everything she wanted to do.   2050
And lord Yvain was more
The master than words could describe.
And then the lady led him
To that hall, full of her knights
And all her men at arms.   2055
And my lord Yvain was so handsome
That they stared at him in wonder,
And rose to their feet as one,
And greeted him, and bowed
To their lord Yvain, and thought: 2060
"This is the man she'll take.
May anyone who stands in his way
Be cursed! He seems a marvellous
Brave knight. The empress of Rome
Would be happy, married to him.   2065
How good it would be if they were promised,

Pledged by their own hands
To be married today or tomorrow!"
And all of them thought the same.
At the head of that hall was a bench   2070
And the lady seated herself there,
Where everyone would be able to see her.
And my lord Yvain began
To seat himself at her feet,
But the lady raised him up   2075
And ordered her steward to speak,
And lift his voice so everyone
There might hear him. And the steward
Began to speak, an obedient
Man with a swift clear tongue: 2080
"My lords!" he said. "We've a war
To face. Each day the king
Is preparing, as fast as he can,
To come and lay waste our lands.
Before another two weeks   2085
It will all have been done, we'll be ruined,
If we haven't some brave defender.
When my lady was married, almost
Seven full years ago,
She did it by your advice.   2090
Now her lord is dead, which hurts her.
All he has is six feet
Of earth, who owned this whole land
And graced it exceedingly well.
What a shame he was here so short   2095
A time. But a woman can't carry
A shield, she can't use a spear.
Better for her, much better,
To marry some worthy knight.
And the need was never greater!   2100
Advise her, all of you, to take

A husband, so the customs of this castle
And this town, in force for more
Than sixty years, can go on."
As these words were spoken they all   2105
Declared it was just what they wanted,
And they threw themselves at her feet.
Her own desire was strengthened,
But she let them beg her to do
As she wished, speaking as if   2110
Against her will, but saying
What she'd say if they'd all opposed her.
So she said: "My lords! Since you wish it,
This knight, who sits beside me,
Has begged me to have him. He wants me.   2115
And he wishes to place himself
At my service, to protect my honor,
And I thank him, as you do also.
To be sure, I've not met him before,
But I've heard him spoken of, and often,   2120
For he's as noble a man as you'll find,
Believe me, and King Urien's son.
And more: his birth is noble,
But he's just as brave as well born,
And blessed with such sense and such chivalry   2125
That no one should block this marriage.
All of you, I think, have heard
Of my lord Yvain, and this
Is he who wishes my hand.
I don't deserve so noble   2130
A husband, but I'll have him, and soon."
And all of them said: "Be wise,
Don't let another day pass
Without making this marriage. How foolish
To let a single hour   2135
Go by without doing anything

So worthy." And they begged her to do
Exactly what she wanted to do,
For Love urged her on,
Though she asked their counsel and advice;   2140
But there's greater honor in taking him
When all of her people advise it.
And nothing they ask displeases her,
But stirs her up and impels her
To let her heart have its way.   2145
A horse half in a gallop
Goes faster, when it feels the spurs.
And with all her barons watching
She gave herself to Yvain.
And he took Laudine de Landuc,   2150
Daughter of Duke Laudunet,
A lord of whom songs are sung,
From the hand of her household priest.
That very same day he married her,
Not waiting a moment to celebrate.   2155
There were plenty of mitres and crosses,
For the lady had summoned all
Her bishops and her abbots. And everyone
There was happy, and many
Were there, and wealth was everywhere,   2160
More than I know how to tell you,
Though I thought on it long and hard.
Better to be silent than speak badly.

And now my lord Yvain
Was master, and the dead man forgotten,   2165
And the man who killed him married
To his wife, and sharing her bed,
And his people happier with their living

Lord than they were with the dead one.
They served him well at his wedding,   2170
Which lasted till the evening before
King Arthur came to see
The wonders of the spring and the stone,
And all his companions with him,
And everyone of all his household,   2175
All gone on this expedition,
No one left behind.
And then my lord Kay spoke up:
"Oh ho! Now what's become
Of Yvain, why isn't he here,   2180
Who boasted—after his dinner—
That he meant to avenge his cousin?
Oh well, he spoke after wine.
I suppose he's run away.
He'll never come back and face us.   2185
That's what comes of such pride.
You have to be brave, daring
To boast of something no one
Would praise, and no one can vouch for,
Except some fawning liar.   2190
Cowards and brave men are different:
A coward sitting near a fire
Puffs out some pretty grand words,
He says the rest of us are fools,
And he thinks that no one knows better.   2195
But a hero would squirm in agony
If someone told stories of the things
He'd done, though he'd really done them.
But how could the coward really
Be wrong to praise himself,   2200
And boast of his strength and his courage?
For who would do it for him?
If he doesn't boast his boasts,

Who would? Even the heralds
Ignore him, proclaiming true heroes   2205
And brushing cowards aside."
And after Sir Kay had spoken,
My lord Gawain answered him:
"Mercy, lord Kay, mercy!
Yvain may not be here,   2210
But who knows what keeps him away?
And truly, he's never stooped
To speaking evil or insulting
You. He's always been courteous."
"My lord!" said Kay. "I'll be quiet.   2215
I'll say nothing more, today,
Since I see I've already offended."
And the king, wanting to see
That rain, spilled a whole bowl
Of water on the magic stone,   2220
And immediately it began to pour.
Nor was it much longer before
My lord Yvain hurried
To the forest, fully armed,
Riding faster than a gallop   2225
On a huge, sleek horse, sturdy
And strong and exceedingly fast.
And Kay, seeing him, determined
That he'd ask for the battle to be his—
For however it might end, he always   2230
Wished to begin the fighting:
If he couldn't be the first to swing
A sword, he'd fly in a rage.
Before anyone else could speak
He begged that the battle might be his.   2235
"Kay!" said the king, "since you want it,
And asked before anyone else,
You shouldn't be refused." Kay thanked him,

Then mounted his horse. And my lord
Yvain was more than happy   2240
To bring him a bit of disgrace,
If he could, for he recognized Kay
At once, from his weapons and armor.
Holding their shields by the straps
They rushed at one another,   2245
Spurring their horses, their spears
Lowered, held firm in their hands
And thrust a little forward.
Holding the leather-covered
Handles they could strike so hard,   2250
When they came together, that both
Spears shattered, splintered
From the tip right up to their hands.
And my lord Yvain struck him
So hard that Kay was swept   2255
From his saddle, somersaulting to the ground,
Which he hit helmet first.
Not wishing to do him more harm,
My lord Yvain quickly
Dismounted and caught up his horse.   2260
And the sight was pleasant to so many
Of the king's knights that they said:
"Ah ha! Now you're lying on the ground,
You who've insulted so many!
And still, it's only right   2265
To pardon you, at least this time,
For it's never happened before."
Meanwhile my lord Yvain
Approached Arthur, leading
The horse by the bridle, intending   2270
To surrender it to the king. And he said:
"My lord! I hand you this horse,
For it would be wrong of me

To keep anything of yours."
"And who are you?" asked the king.   2275
"I'd never know, unless
I heard your name or saw you
Without your armor." And then
My lord Yvain told him
His name, and Kay was overwhelmed   2280
With shame, crushed, crestfallen,
That he'd called Yvain a coward.
But the others were delighted, deeply
Pleased by the honor Yvain
Had won. And even the king   2285
Was pleased, and my lord Gawain
Was a hundred times happier than anyone
Else, for he cherished that friendship
More than that of any
Knight he knew. And the king   2290
Asked Yvain to please
Tell them, if he would, just how
This adventure had come about,
For he found himself immensely
Curious to understand it all.   2295
So he urged Yvain to speak.
And Yvain told them everything,
All the good will and the help
The girl had given him, steering
His way through the entire story,   2300
Forgetting nothing. And then
He invited the king, and with him
All his knights, to come
To stay at his home. They would do him
Great honor, and bring him much joy,   2305
If they'd agree to be his guests.
And the king said he'd gladly
Come for an entire week,

To honor him, and please him, and share
His company. And Yvain thanked him,   2310
And they stayed where they were no longer.
Mounting their horses, they took
The shortest road to his castle.
And my lord Yvain sent
A squire to go before them,   2315
Carrying a hunting falcon,
So his lady might not be surprised
And all their people might make
Their houses beautiful, for the king's
Coming. And the lady, when she heard,   2320
Was delighted that the king was coming.
And no one who heard the news
Was anything less than pleased.
And the lady sent for them all
And asked them to go and meet him,   2325
And they neither quarreled nor grumbled,
But set out cheerfully, all of them
Anxious to do as she wished.

Riding their huge Spanish horses
They went to meet the British   2330
King, greeting with great courtesy
Royal Arthur and then
Everyone who travelled with him.
"Welcome," they cried, "to this party,
Brave knights all! Blessed   2335
Be he who leads you here
And gives us so many good guests!"
The town rang with happiness
Because of the king's coming.

They brought out their silken sheets   2340
And hung them in front of their houses,
And put out tapestries to walk on,
And hung them along the streets,
All for the king, as they waited.
And they readied something else: 2345
Canopies across their streets
To keep off the heat of the sun.
Church bells rang, horns blew,
And trumpets, making so much noise
That God's own thunder could never   2350
Have been heard. Girls danced for him,
And flutes and pipes played,
And tambourines, and cymbals, and drums.
And elsewhere, nimble young men
Did their part, dancing and leaping—   2355
Happiness ruling them all.
And with this sort of celebration
They gave the king a fitting
Welcome. And out came their lady,
Wearing a queenly gown,   2360
A dress of brand new ermine,
And on her head a crown
Rich with red rubies, and nowhere
On her face could one see concern,
But so much happiness and laughter   2365
That she seems to me to be lovelier
Than any immortal goddess.
And her people crowded around her,
And each and all of them cried:
"Welcome to the king, the master   2370
Of all worldly lords and kings!"
The king had barely begun
To answer when he saw the lady
Coming to hold his bridle.

And thinking he would not wait,   2375
As soon as he saw her approaching
He quickly dismounted from his horse.
And the lady greeted him, and said:
"A hundred thousand welcomes
To my lord the king, and blessings   2380
On his nephew, my lord Gawain."
"And to you," answered the king,
"Lovely creature, I wish
Great joy and great good luck!"
Then the king hugged her to him,   2385
Nobly and with spirit, and the lady
Threw her arms around him.
But how she welcomed them all
Is hardly worth telling: no one
Has ever heard of guests   2390
Granted such a welcome,
With such honor and so much attention.
I could describe a good deal of happiness,
But why waste words? I shall only
Mention a friendship struck,   2395
Entirely in private, no one
To see or to hear, between
The moon and the sun. And who
Do you think I mean to refer to?
He who was lord of all knights   2400
More famous than any, should certainly
Be called the sun. I speak,
Of course, of my lord Gawain,
Who shed his lustre on the world
Of chivalry exactly as the sun   2405
Rising in the morning opens
His rays and breathes his famous
Warmth everywhere he's seen.
And she I have called the moon

Could be called nothing else, because   2410
Of her lofty wisdom, and her courtesy.
And nevertheless that's not
The only reason for calling her
Moon, for her name was Lunette.

The girl's name was Lunette,   2415
Gracious, brunette, exceedingly
Wise and knowing and quick.
The better Gawain knew her
The better he thought of her, and loved her,
And declared her his friend, she   2420
Who had saved his comrade and friend
From certain death, and he gave her
A pledge of service and support.
And she told him how hard it had been
To get around her mistress,   2425
To bring her to marrying my lord
Yvain, and how she had sheltered
Yvain from the hands of those
Who would have killed him. He'd been
Right there, but they couldn't see him.   2430
And Gawain laughed with delight
At her story, and said: "My dear
Young lady, I hereby give you
Whatever sort of knight
I may be, for whatever use   2435
I may be. Don't exchange me for anyone
Else you think may be better.
I am yours—and you shall be mine,
Now and forever." "I thank you,
Kind sir!" she agreed.   2440
                    And while

These two were becoming acquainted,
There were others talking of love.
There may have been ninety ladies
In attendance, each of them beautiful,
And gracious, and well-bred, and clever,   2445
And wise, and all well-born.
It was easy to find entertainment,
Hugging and kissing and talking
And simply watching, and sitting
Beside them at night. That much   2450
Was easy, and that much they had.
And Yvain was immensely happy,
Having the king as his guest.
And the lady so honored everyone,
Separately and all together,   2455
That fools might have thought it was love
Drawing her on, and love
She offered them all. They're simple
Idiots, and deserve the name,
Thinking a lady is in love   2460
Because she is gracious and polite
To some blockhead, and makes him happy,
And hugs him. It's fools who are happy
With pretty words. There's nothing
Difficult about fooling a fool.   2465

A week went by, spent
In pleasure and delight. The woods
And the river opened their arms
To anyone who wanted to enjoy them.
And those who wished to see   2470
The lands my lord Yvain
Had conquered, that came with the lady

He'd won, could easily amuse
Themselves at one of the neighboring
Castles, a mile or two off.   2475
And the king, when he'd made his visit
And wished to stay no longer,
Got ready to say his farewells.
But his courtiers had spent the week
Determined, if they could, to take   2480
My lord Yvain home
With them. They'd begged and argued
And worked as hard as they could.
"What?" said Gawain. "There are men
Who aren't the men they were   2485
Once they're married. Not you!
By Mary, Mother of Heaven,
The devil with anyone who marries
And goes slack! A beautiful lady
Should make us better, as friend   2490
Or as wife. No one should be loved
Who isn't worth it. And you,
Surely you'll regret her love
If it makes you worthless. For a woman
Can just as easily fall out   2495
Of love—and there's nothing wrong
In hating anyone who turns worthless
As soon as he's lord of the realm.
It's now that you need to prove
Yourself! Take the bit in your teeth: 2500
We ought to go jousting, you
And I, so no one can call you
Jealous. You shouldn't be lazy,
But throw yourself into tournaments,
Take on the world, and with pleasure,   2505
Whatever it costs you! Lying
Around will change you for the worse.

Now really, you've got to come,
For I'll come with you. Be careful,
My friend, that we don't fall out,   2510
And cease to be comrades! It won't
Be any fault of mine.
I'm here. How strange to fall
In love with endless ease.
Things grow sweeter when you're forced   2515
To delay them, and a little thing
That we're obliged to wait for is better
Than some great thing that we always have.
The pleasures of love, when they come to us
Late, are like fire in a green   2520
Log, burning hotter and longer
And keeping their heat better
For taking so long to light.
Habits can grow on us,
Can get hard to give up. We can want to   2525
And find that we can't. And surely,
My comrade, my friend, I have
No lover like yours, so beautiful,
So good. By God and all
The saints in heaven, if I had her   2530
You couldn't pry me away!
I'd be her fool and her slave.
I know: a man can give
Advice he couldn't follow
Himself, just like the preachers,   2535
All of them lying swindlers,
But teaching what's right, and speaking it,
Though they never do it themselves."

And Gawain said so much

And so urgently, and begged him so hard,   2540
That Yvain agreed, but said
He needed to speak to his wife,
To see if she minded his going,
For whether it was wise or foolish
He'd never leave her and return   2545
To Britain without her consent.
So he took his wife aside
(Who had no way of knowing
What he wanted) and said: "Dear lady!
My very heart and soul,   2550
My treasure, my joy, and my happiness,
For your honor, and also for mine,
Promise me something!" And the lady
Immediately agreed, not knowing
What he meant to ask, and she said: 2555
"Sweet sir! I am yours to command,
Whatever the favor may be."
And so my lord Yvain
Asked her to permit him to escort
Arthur home, and then   2560
Go tourneying, so no one could call him
A coward. And she said: "I agree—
But only till a day we shall fix.
My love will turn to hate,
Believe me—for it's true, and it's certain—   2565
If you stay too long and stay past
The day I shall tell you. And this
Is the truth: I'll tell you no lies.
You can break your word. I'll keep mine.
If you wish to have my love,   2570
And if you think well of me,
Make up your mind to be back
At the very latest a year
And a week from the feast of Saint John,

For this is the eighth day since that feast.   2575
If you're not here with me
On precisely that day you'll have lost
My love, like a checkmated king."
    My lord Yvain wept
And sighed and found it hard to say,   2580
"Lady! It's a long way off.
If I were a dove I could come
And be with you as often as I liked,
And as much as I liked. And I pray
To God, if it pleases Him,   2585
Not to keep me too long
Away from you. Sometimes a man
Means to hurry, but can't know
The future. Who knows what will happen?
I may become ill. I may   2590
Be held prisoner. Events may detain me.
I think you're wrong, and unjust,
Not to exclude at least
Physical impossibility."
"Sir!" she said, "I'll grant that.   2595
And still, I swear to you, if our Lord
Keeps you from death, nothing
Will stand in your way as long
As you never forget me. Here:
Put on your finger this ring   2600
Of mine. I loan it to you.
And let me tell you exactly
What sort of stone it is.
No true and loyal lover
Can be captured, or lose any blood,   2605
Nor have any evil come to him,
As long as he wears it and holds it
Dear and remembers his beloved.
He turns as hard as iron.

It serves him as shield and armor.   2610
No knight has ever had it
From my hand. I give it to you
Only because of my love."
And now Yvain had his freedom,
But wept at the thought of taking it.—   2615
But the king would not wait for anything,
No matter what anyone said.
Indeed, he grew impatient
To have the horses led in,
Bridled and ready to leave.   2620
And whatever he wanted was what everyone
Did: the horses were led in,
And all that was left was to mount them.
Should I really tell you how my lord
Yvain said his farewells,   2625
And the kisses he took, and the kisses
He gave, sprinkled with tears
And scented with sweetness? Should I tell you
About the king, how the lady
Herself escorted him, her maids   2630
In waiting with her, and all
Her ladies, and all her knights?
It would take too long to tell.
When he saw how the lady wept,
The king begged her to come   2635
No further, but go back to her home.
He urged her so seriously, and so hard,
That she and her people turned back.

How hard it was for my lord
Yvain to leave his wife!   2640
He rode off without his heart.

His body might follow the king,
But his heart could not be led.
She who held it, joined
To her own, was she who stayed home,   2645
And nothing could pry it loose.
No body without a heart
Can possibly live long. No one
Has ever seen such a marvel
As a living body with no heart.   2650
And yet this wonder came true:
The body kept its life
But kept it without its heart,
Which would not go with its body.
The heart had a good place to stay in,   2655
And the body lived on, hoping
Its heart would return, and making
A strange sort of heart out of hope,
Though hope is so often a traitor,
A breaker of promises. And Yvain   2660
Will never know in advance
Just when hope will betray him,
For all he needs to do
Is stay a day later
Than agreed on, and his wife will be hard   2665
To talk into peace and a truce.
And I think he will stay too late:
For Gawain won't let him go,
Once the two of them have begun
To travel about, fighting   2670
Wherever tournaments can be found.
And indeed, as the year went by,
Yvain had such success
Everywhere he went, that Gawain
Was determined to honor him, and made him   2675
Linger so long that a year

Had gone, and enough of the next one
With it, and Assumption had arrived,
And the month of August, and the king
Was holding his court at Chester,   2680
And the evening before they'd come
From a tournament where my lord Yvain
Had entered and fought and taken
All the prizes. And the story
Told of those times tells   2685
That lord Yvain and his comrade
Were unwilling to take lodgings in town,
But had their tents pitched
Outside the city, and held court—
For they never attended the king's   2690
Court. The king came to theirs,
For their knights were better and far
More numerous than his. And Arthur
Was seated among them when all
Of a sudden Yvain was struck   2695
By an overwhelming thought,
A thought that surprised him more
Than anything he'd thought of since leaving
His wife. He realized all
At once that he'd broken his promise   2700
And stayed beyond the time
They'd agreed. He could barely keep
From crying, but shame held back
His tears. And while deep in thought
He saw a girl approaching him,   2705
Mounted on a black horse
With spotted white feet, and riding
Swiftly. She dismounted at the tent,
But no one helped her, and no one
Came forward to take her horse.   2710
And as soon as she was able to locate

The king, she dropped the cloak
From her shoulders, and let it fall,
And came into the tent, and straight
To the king, and stood in front of him,   2715
And said that her mistress sent greetings
To Arthur, and also to Gawain,
And to everyone except Yvain,
For he was disloyal, and a traitor,
And a liar, and a deceiver, who'd deserted   2720
His wife and betrayed her. "She knows
How little his lying is worth,
Pretending to be a faithful
Lover, but truly a treacherous
Thief. And he's cheated my mistress,   2725
Who'd expected nothing but good,
And never believed he'd come
Only to steal her heart. For those
Who truly love are not thieves.
And yet there are men, and we call   2730
Them thieves, who cheat at love,
But really know nothing about it.
A lover takes his beloved's
Heart, but he never steals it,
He watches it, he keeps it safe   2735
From thieves, who pretend to be honest.
But these hypocritical thieves
And traitors always struggle
To steal hearts that are worthless to them.
A lover, wherever he goes,   2740
Cherishes that heart, and returns it.
But Yvain has killed my mistress:
She thought he would care for her heart,
And bring it back to her, before
A year had gone by. Yvain!   2745
You've forgotten it all, you couldn't

Be bothered to remember a thing.
You were pledged to return to my mistress
In exactly a year. She gave you,
And graciously, all the time   2750
Till the feast of Saint John, and you,
You've shown her such contempt
That you've never thought of her at all.
There in her room my mistress
Counted every day,   2755
For lovers live in anxiety,
And they're never able to sleep,
But every night they add up
The days, as they come and go.
Do you know how it is with lovers?   2760
They watch the days and the seasons.
She accuses you neither with no reason
Nor too soon, though nothing I say
Is meant for some judge's ears.
The only thing I say   2765
Is that she who married you to my mistress
Has betrayed her. Yvain! My mistress
Disowns you. She sends me to tell you
Never to come back, but only
Return her ring. I   2770
Who stand here before you will carry it
Back to her. Surrender it now!
You're pledged to give it back."

And Yvain could not speak, could not answer,
Deprived of his senses and his tongue.   2775
But the girl came forward, and pulled
The ring from his finger, and then
Commended the king to God,

And all the others, except him
Whom she left in deep distress.—   2780
And his sorrow grew all the time,
Making him suffer from everything
He heard and everything he saw.
He wished he'd been sent away
To some savage land, all alone,   2785
Where no one would know him, or find him,
And neither man nor woman
Would know anything more about him
Than if he'd fallen in some abyss.
There was nothing he hated as much   2790
As himself, and no one to comfort him
In the death he'd chosen for himself.
And still he would choose to go mad
Rather than not take revenge
On himself, for taking away   2795
His happiness. He withdrew from his fellow
Knights, and feared for his sanity.
And they ignored him, left him
Entirely alone, as he chose.
And they knew how little he cared   2800
For their doings, and their words, and for them.
And then he wandered far
From all the pavilions and tents.
And such a storm broke
In his skull that he lost his senses,   2805
And he tore at his skin and his clothes,
And crossed meadows and fields, and left
His squires and his men so uncertain
That they had no idea where he was.
And they hunted everywhere, seeking him   2810
Wherever there were knights living,
And in hedgerows, and in orchards, but nowhere
They looked was where he was.

Running, and running, he'd gone
Until near an enclosure he found   2815
A boy carrying a bow
And five hunting arrows,
Large ones, and sharp, and he had
Sense enough left that he took
The boy's bow, and took the arrows   2820
The boy had with him. But nothing
He had done stayed in his mind:
He remembered none of it. And then
He lay in wait for the forest
Animals, and killed them, and ate   2825
Their flesh completely raw.
And that was how he lived
In the woods, like a madman or a savage,
Until he came on a squat
And tiny house that belonged   2830
To a hermit, who was clearing ground
For a garden. And seeing Yvain
All naked, he knew at once
That the man's mind was not right,
Which was true, of course. And the hermit   2835
Was terribly afraid, and shut
Himself in his tiny house.
But the good man took a bit
Of his bread, and some pure water,
And for charity's sake set them   2840
Outside, on a narrow window.
And Yvain came, hungering
For the bread, which he snatched up and bolted.
He'd never in his life tasted
Such hard, coarse stuff, and sour,   2845
Baked out of grain worth
A couple of pennies, at most,
Baked from rotten barley

And straw, or more like husks
Or shells than cake, mouldy   2850
All through, and dry as bark.
But hunger hurt him, and forced him,
And he thought it tasted like porridge,
For hunger is a lovely, well-made
Sauce for any food.   2855
And he finished every bite
Of the hermit's bread, and enjoyed it,
And drank some good cold water.
And after he'd eaten he went back
To the wood, and hunted deer.   2860
And seeing him leave, the good man,
Hiding under his roof,
Prayed for God to preserve
And protect him, and keep Yvain
Away. But no one, no matter   2865
How crack-brained, thinks of staying
Away from a place where he's treated
Well. So as long as the frenzy
Was on him not a day would pass
But Yvain would bring the hermit   2870
Some wild beast, and leave it
At his door. And that was his life.
And the good man made it his business
To skin most of the carcasses
And cook the meat, and whenever   2875
The madman wanted to eat
And drink there was bread and water
Waiting on the window, and so
He ate and he drank, his meat
Unsalted, and no pepper, and his drink   2880
Cold water fresh from a spring.
And the good man made it his business
To sell the hides and buy bread

Baked of good barley or oats
Or wheat, so Yvain was well   2885
Supplied with both bread and meat,
Which could last him a long, long time.
Until one day two girls,
And their mistress with them, in whose service
Both were engaged, found him   2890
Sleeping in the forest. And one of them,
As soon as she saw the naked
Man, dismounted and ran
And stared at him hard, trying
To find something about him   2895
From which she might know his name.
Had Yvain been dressed as he'd always
Been, many and many
A day, in rich and noble
Robes, she'd have known him at once.   2900
But it took her time to know him,
And she stared and stared until,
At last, she became aware
Of a scar on his face, just such
A scar as she'd seen on the face   2905
Of my lord Yvain, and she knew it,
For she'd seen it often. And the scar
Made it all clear: it was him,
She had no doubt. But what
A wondrous thing to behold   2910
What he'd come to, to find him in the woods,
Naked and poor. She watched him,
Amazed, crossing herself,
But neither touched nor awoke him.
She took her horse, and remounted,   2915
And went back to the others, and weeping
Told them everything she'd seen.
Should I stop to tell you all the grief

She showed? I don't know. In any
Event, she said to her mistress,   2920
Weeping: "My lady! I've found
Yvain, the most famous knight
In the world, and the best. But what sin
Has stricken this noble man
I haven't the faintest idea.   2925
I expect he's experienced some sorrow,
And it's brought him to this. It's easy
For grief to drive you mad.
And anyone can see it, and know it:
The man's quite out of his mind.   2930
For he'd never permit himself
To be seen so shamefully if he hadn't
Lost his senses. Would God
Had restored him exactly as he was,
In the best of health and mind,   2935
And made him willing and able
To come to your aid! For Count
Alier, with whom you're at war,
Has launched a bitter attack.
But the war between you two   2940
Would be quickly settled in your favor
If God gave you the blessed
Good fortune to have him restored
To his senses, and led him to take
Your side in this time of need."   2945
Said the lady: "Be careful! For surely,
If he doesn't escape us, I think
That with God's assistance we may
Be able to drive all this frenzy
And storm from his head, and return him   2950
To himself. But we'll have to hurry.
I remember a magic ointment,
Given me by Morgan le Fay,

Who told me no fever in the brain
Could resist it. It will cure them all."   2955
And at once they headed back
To her castle, not more than half
A mile distant (the way they measure
Miles in that country, as compared
To us, calling two miles   2960
One, and four miles two).
Yvain stayed alone, sleeping,
And the lady hunted for the ointment.
She went to her linen chest,
Unlocked it, took out a box   2965
And gave it to the girl, warning her
Not to use it too freely.
His temples and his forehead should be rubbed:
There was no need to use it elsewhere.
Only his temples required   2970
The ointment; the rest should be kept.
There was nothing wrong with any
Part of him except his brain.
And she told her to bring a fur-lined
Cloak, and scarlet silk clothes.   2975
And the girl took them, and her right hand
Led a fine horse. And she added
A shirt and some well-spun breeches,
And beautiful new stockings, all
Her own. She rode off quickly,   2980
With all these things, and found him
Still sleeping, there where she'd left him.
She put the horses in a sheltered
Spot, and tied them exceedingly
Carefully and well, then carrying   2985
The clothes and the ointment she walked
Where he lay asleep on the ground.
And it took great courage to approach

The madman as she did, meaning
To touch and to handle him. Then she took   2990
The ointment and rubbed him with it
Until none was left in the box,
So anxious to cure him that she rubbed him
Everywhere, till she'd used it all,
Paying no attention to her mistress'   2995
Warning—indeed, completely
Forgetting it. She rubbed in more
Than could ever be needed, but hardly
Enough, in her opinion.
She rubbed from his temples and his forehead   3000
Right down to his toes. She rubbed
His temples and all his body
So well, in that bright warm sun,
That all his frenzy and his sadness
Slipped right out of his brain.   3005
But she was foolish to anoint his body:
It was hardly necessary. And yet,
I suspect she'd have done the same thing
If the box had held five times
As much. Then carrying away   3010
The box, she went to rest
Near the horses, but carefully didn't
Take the clothing: if God
Restored him to his senses, she wanted him
To see it, and take it, and wear it.   3015
Hiding herself behind
A huge oak, she waited till he'd slept
All he wanted, and woke, and was cured,
His mind and his memory recovered.
And seeing himself naked   3020
As ivory, he was terribly ashamed,
But it would have been worse had he known
Everything he'd done. But all

He knew was his nakedness. And he saw
The new clothes, and was deeply astonished: 3025
How had that gown come
To be there? Who could have brought it?
But the sight of his naked flesh
Oppressed him, and bewildered him, and he said
To himself: I am dead, betrayed,   3030
If anyone finds me, and I'm wearing
Nothing, and they know who I am.
And as he spoke he got dressed
And looked toward the forest, watching
To see if anyone came.   3035
He tried to stand up, unaided,
But could not; neither could he walk.
And seeing that he needed help,
And knew it, and was ready to accept it,
Overcome with such intense weakness   3040
That he could scarcely stay on his feet,
The girl decided not to wait
Any longer, but got up on her horse
And rode on by him, pretending
Not to know he was there. And knowing   3045
How badly he needed help,
Someone to bring him to some refuge
And the chance to recover his strength,
And not caring who helped him, he forced
Himself to call to her, as loudly   3050
As he could. And the girl obligingly
Looked all around, as if
Unable to understand what was happening.
And apparently bewildered, she went this way
And then that, not wishing to head   3055
Straight toward him. And he started to call her
Again: "Girl! This way!
This way!" And she let her horse

Go slowly toward him. And pretending
As she had, she made him think   3060
She'd never seen him before
And hadn't the faintest idea
Who he was. It was wisely and courteously
Done. And reaching him, she said:
"Knight! What is it you wish,   3065
Calling me so very urgently?"
"Ah!" he said, "wise girl!
Somehow, by some ill luck,
I find myself in this wood.
For the sake of God and your faith   3070
In Him, I beg you, help me,
Lend me, give me that horse
You're leading behind you." "Most willingly,
Dear sir. But come with me,
There where I'm going." "Which is where?"   3075
He said. "Out of this forest,
To a nearby castle." "Girl!
Tell me: have you some need
Of my service as a knight?" "Yes,"
She answered. "But it seems to me   3080
You're not in good health. For the next
Two weeks, at least, you ought
To be resting. Take the reins
Of this horse I'm leading, and come,
We'll ride to the castle where I live."   3085
And wishing to do exactly
What she asked, he took it, and mounted,
And off they went. And they came
To a bridge across a swift-flowing
Stream, and the girl threw in   3090
The empty box she was carrying.
She meant to excuse herself
To her mistress, for using too much

Of the ointment. She would tell her that as luck
Had it, passing across   3095
The bridge she'd dropped the box—
Her horse had stumbled under her,
And the box had slipped from her hand,
And what's more, she'd almost fallen
After it herself, and that   3100
Would have been a greater loss.
She meant to concoct this lie
As soon as she stood in her lady's
Presence. So they rode on together,
Until they came to the castle,   3105
And the lady gladly welcomed
My lord Yvain, and as soon
As she could she got the girl
Alone and asked for her box
And her magic ointment, and the girl   3110
Told her exactly the lie
She'd invented, not daring to tell her
The truth. And her mistress was fiercely
Angry, and said: "This
Is a very serious loss.   3115
I haven't a doubt in the world
It will never be found. Never.
When a thing is gone, it's gone;
I shall have to do without it.
How often we wish for something,   3120
And instead of good it turns out
Bad. And I, who expected
Good fortune and joy of this knight,
Have lost my best and most cherished
Possession of all. Ah well: 3125
Despite this, I wish you to serve him
Well; give him what he needs."
"Ah, my lady! How well

You've spoken! How vulgar it would be
To turn one misfortune into two."   3130

They said no more of the box,
And did everything they could to help
My lord Yvain, bathing him
And washing his hair, and having it
Clipped, and his face shaved—   3135
For you could have plucked handfuls
Of hair from his face. There was nothing
He wanted that he did not have:
If he asked for armor, he got it;
If he asked for a horse, they immediately   3140
Gave him a great strong beast,
And a beauty. And he stayed there until,
One Tuesday, the count Alier
And all his men came to town,
And set fires, and plundered, and robbed.   3145
And those who lived there mounted
Their horses and took up their weapons
And armed or not they went out
To attack their attackers, who for their part
Were far too proud to flee,   3150
But allowed the defenders to come to them.
And Yvain rushed at them, and struck at them,
Having rested so long that his strength
Had returned. And he hit so hard,
Right through a knight's shield, that according   3155
To my sources he tumbled both knight
And horse together in a heap,
From which that knight would never
Rise again, for his heart

Was ruptured, deep in his guts,   3160
And his backbone was crushed. And then
Yvain drew back a bit,
Before he attacked once more,
And protecting himself with his shield
Began to sweep the invaders   3165
Away. And it would have been hard
To count from one to four
Before you could have seen him
Cast down four knights, quickly
And completely. And those who were with him   3170
Were suddenly encouraged, and turned
Into warriors, for many a mean-spirited
Wretch, and a coward, seeing
A brave man take on a difficult
Struggle right in front of his eyes,   3175
Is attacked by shame, overwhelmed,
And throws his miserable heart
Out of his body and acquires
A true knight's spirit, brave
And noble and strong. And all   3180
The defenders became brave, and each of them
Held his ground well, there
In that battle, and fought with honor.
And the lady, standing high
In her castle tower, saw   3185
The battle and the assault, the struggle
For land and for right, saw more
Than enough men lying on the ground,
Some wounded, some dead, some
Of her own men, and some of the enemy's,   3190
But more of the others than hers,
For my lord Yvain, courteous
And brave and good, made them
Beg for his mercy, like a falcon

Hunting freshwater ducks.   3195
And those who stood on the castle
Walls, men and women
Alike, watching the fighting,
All said: "What a splendid soldier!
How he makes his enemies surrender,   3200
How fiercely he attacks them! He rushes
Among them like a lion hunting
Deer, impelled by pain
And hunger. And because of him all
Our other knights are braver   3205
And bolder—and indeed, if it weren't
For him, and only for him,
No spear would ever have been splintered,
No sword lifted and swung.
Love and cherish so noble   3210
A man, when there's one to be found.
Just see how he proves himself,
Just see how he holds our lines
Together, see how his spear
And his sword are splashed with blood,   3215
See how he chases them down,
See how he drives them off,
How he comes and goes and goes at them,
How he steps back, when he must,
But only for a little rest,   3220
And quickly back into battle.
See how he wins his honor,
Not worrying about his shield,
Letting them cut it to bits.
He shows them no mercy—none!   3225
See how eagerly he gives them
Back the blows they give him.
If all the Argonne forest
Were cut down to make his spears,

There'd be none of them left by nightfall,   3230
For all of the spearheads they give him
He breaks—and calls for more.
Just see how he swings his sword,
When he needs to use it. Roland
Himself never slaughtered so many,   3235
Slashing with Durendal, his sword,
Not even at Roncevaux or in Spain!
If only he had with him some comrades
As good as himself, that villain
Who's given us such cause for complaint   3240
Would be beaten, today, and he'd run—
Or be utterly shamed, if he stayed."
And they said that anyone who'd given
Her love to such a man
Would be blessed—a man so powerful   3245
In battle, recognized over all
Other men, like a torch among candles,
Or the moon against the stars,
Or the sun against the moon.
And each of them said to the other   3250
That they wished as hard as they could,
Seeing his strength and his skill,
That he were married to their lady
And ruled their people and their land.

So everyone who saw him praised him,   3255
And simply told the truth—
For he'd laid into their enemies
So well that one outran
The other. And he followed them fiercely,
And all his comrades with him,   3260
All of them feeling as safe

At his side as if enclosed
In a high, a thick stone wall.
The chase was long, and hard,
Until the hunted grew weary,   3265
And the hunters cut them to pieces,
And cut the guts from their horses,
And the living rolled on the dead,
Stabbing at each other, and killing.
The slaughter was ghastly, was murderous.   3270
And still the Count kept running,
And lord Yvain ran after him,
Never faltering at his heels.
And on they ran, until
At the foot of a steep hill   3275
He caught him, close to the entrance
Of one of the Count's forts.
And so the Count was captured,
And no one could possibly help him,
And without a great many words   3280
He surrendered to my lord Yvain.
For as soon as he had him in his hands,
And they stood alone, man to man,
There was no way the Count could escape,
Or hide, or defend himself.   3285
And so he swore to surrender
To the lady of Noroison,
And make himself her prisoner,
And accept such peace as she gave him.
And after he'd sworn his surrender,   3290
Yvain obliged him to give up
His helmet, drop the shield
From his neck, and hand over his sword.
And honor had come to Yvain,
Capturing the Count and giving him   3295
Into his enemies' hands,

Who made no secret of their pleasure.
And the news travelled before them,
Coming to town before
They arrived. And everyone went out   3300
To meet them, and the lady first
Of all. And Yvain held
His prisoner by the hand, and gave him
To her. And the Count gave in
At once to everything she asked,   3305
And swore the most solemn oaths
To keep his promises. And the pledges
He gave her, and swore to, promised
Eternal peace between them,
And compensation for her losses   3310
(Providing she offered good proof),
And reconstruction of all
The houses he'd levelled to the ground.
And when all these things were arranged
Exactly as the lady deserved,   3315
Yvain requested permission
To leave her. She'd never have agreed,
Had he been willing to have her
As his mistress, or take her as his wife.
And Yvain forbade them to escort him   3320
Or follow him a single step,
But left them as fast as he could:
Nothing they said persuaded him.
And off he went, retracing
His path, and leaving the lady   3325
Miserable, though at first he'd made her
So happy. And the happier he'd made her,
The more he distressed and afflicted her,
Refusing to stay any longer,
For she wished she could honor him, she'd gladly   3330
Have made him, if only he'd consent,

Lord of everything she owned,
Or given him some immense reward,
In return for the service he'd rendered her,
As huge a reward as he'd take.   3335
But he wished to listen to no one,
No man and no woman. And he left
The lady and her knights, all of them
Deeply unhappy, no one
Able to keep him among them.   3340

And then my lord Yvain,
Thoughtful, travelled through
A deep wood, and there he heard
A great loud cry, and hurried
Directly toward it, following   3345
The sound. And when he arrived
At that place, he saw a clearing
In the forest, and a lion, and a snake,
Which had the lion by the tail
And was burning him up, consuming him   3350
With sheets of intense hot flame.
My lord Yvain didn't waste
Much time watching this wonder.
He asked himself which
Of the two he ought to help,   3355
Then told himself to help
The lion, for a venomous and treacherous
Beast should not be permitted
To do evil. And snakes are venomous,
And fire leaps from their mouths,   3360
Overflowing with treachery. And so
My lord Yvain thought
Of killing the snake first.

He drew his sword and stepped forward,
Holding his shield in front of   3365
His face, to keep the flames
From harming him, fire pouring
From its jaws, gaping wider
Than a boiler. And then, if the lion
Attacked him, there'd be plenty of fighting.   3370
But whatever happened, he'd made up
His mind to help the lion,
For pity urged him on,
Begging him to rescue that noble,
Highborn beast. And swinging   3375
His sword, which cut so smoothly,
He began to attack the snake,
Cutting him clean through to the ground,
Then slicing him in half, and striking him
Over and over, till he'd chopped him   3380
To tiny pieces. But because
The snake had gripped the lion's
Tail in his poisonous teeth,
He was forced to chop a piece
From the tail, but he cut only   3385
As much as he had to, and he had
No choice, there was no other way.
And when he'd freed the lion
He was sure the animal would attack him,
And he'd have to fight, but fighting   3390
Was not what the lion intended.
Now hear what that lion did!
Showing his nobility and goodness,
He began to make it clear
That he surrendered himself to Yvain: 3395
Placing his front feet together,
He stood erect on his hind legs
And bowed his face toward the earth.

And then he knelt again,
And his face was wet all over   3400
With humble tears. And my lord
Yvain knew without doubt
That the lion was offering him thanks
And humbling himself before
His deliverer, who in killing the snake   3405
Had saved him from certain death.
And Yvain was deeply pleased.
He dried his sword, stained
With the snake's venom, and its filth,
Then thrust it back in its scabbard   3410
And went on his way. And the lion
Began to walk beside him,
Determined never to leave,
But always to go where he went,
To serve and protect him. And so   3415
He set out in front of Yvain,
Until as he trotted along
The wind blew him the scent
Of wild beasts grazing, and hunger
And natural instinct set him   3420
Running and hunting for his food:
And that was simply nature's
Way, he did what he had to.
He'd begin to follow a trail,
As if to show his master   3425
That he'd found the scent of some wild
Animal, met it on the wind.
Then, watching Yvain, he would stop,
Wanting to please him, not wanting
In any way to go   3430
Against his wishes. And Yvain
Noted the look on his face,
Which showed him that the lion was waiting.

He saw it, and knew what it meant:
If he stayed where he was, the lion   3435
Would stay; if he followed, the lion
Would catch the game he had scented.
And Yvain urged him on,
Shouting as he'd shout to a pack
Of hounds. And the lion immediately   3440
Sniffed out the trail, and followed it,
Knowing exactly what it meant,
And hardly running a bow-shot
Away before he saw
A single deer, grazing   3445
In a valley. He'll catch it, if he can,
And he does, at the very first leap,
And drinks its fresh hot blood.
And after the kill, he put
The deer on his back, and brought it   3450
Where he saw his master coming,
And Yvain felt such a rush
Of affection that he took him to be
His companion through all the days
Of his life, so great was his love.   3455
    And now it was nearly night,
And Yvain decided to sleep there,
And to cut as much as he wanted
To eat from the dead deer.
And so he began to skin it,   3460
Splitting along the side,
Then slicing a steak from the loin,
And using his flint to strike
A spark, he kindled dry
Brushwood, then pierced his steak   3465
On a wooden spit and set
To roasting it through and through.
But he took no pleasure in eating it

Without bread or wine or salt,
No table cloth, no carving set—nothing.   3470
As he ate, the lion lay
Motionless beside him, watching him
The whole time, until
He'd eaten as much as he wanted
Of his steak, and could eat no more.   3475
And whatever was left of the deer
The lion ate to the bone.
Yvain then slept through the night,
His head resting on his shield,
Sleeping as well as he could,   3480
And the lion showed such good sense
That he stayed awake, carefully
Guarding the horse, who grazed
In the grass, which wasn't very good.

In the morning they left together,   3485
And as far as I know they began
To lead exactly the sort
Of existence they'd shared that night,
And so it went, for almost
Two weeks, until they chanced on   3490
The spring under the pine tree.
And there my lord Yvain
Almost went mad again,
Approaching that spring, and the stone,
And the chapel that stood beside them.   3495
He sighed a thousand sad
And weary sighs, then fainted,
And his sword slipped from its scabbard
And its well-sharpened point nicked him

On the cheek, above the neck,   3500
Cut him through the rings of his mail-shirt.
No metal mesh is perfect:
The tip of the sword slipped through
His shining mail and slit
His skin, and blood fell.   3505
The lion thought he saw
His lord and master dead.
No one could ever find words
To tell of sadder or louder
Noises than he started to make!   3510
He rolled on the ground, and roared,
And decided to kill himself
With the sword he thought had killed
His loving master. And taking
The sword in his teeth he propped it   3515
Erect on a fallen tree,
And steadied its hilt on another
Tree, so it could not slip
When he ran his chest against it.
He'd nearly done what he meant   3520
To do, when Yvain came to,
And the lion swerved aside
In his desperate rush at death,
Charging like a wild boar
Who pays no attention, but just runs.   3525
My lord Yvain lay near
The stone, where he'd fallen in his faint,
And as he recovered bitterly
Accused himself for exceeding
His year's leave and making   3530
His lady hate him: "Why can't he
Kill himself, this miserable
Creature from whom joy has fled?
Oh lord, why don't I do it?

How can I stand here and see
These things that belong to my wife?   3535
Why does my soul remain
In this body, this miserable home?
It would never know such agony
If it had gone away. Hating
And blaming and despising myself   3540
As I do is what I deserve.
Whoever loses happiness
And comfort because of his own
Wrongs should hate himself
To death. He should kill himself.   3545
And I, alone, unseen,
Why do I spare myself?
And haven't I seen this lion,
Who felt such grief for me
That he was ready to set my sword   3550
Against his chest and thrust it
In? Should I be afraid
Of death, who changed joy to sadness?
Joy has left me. Joy?
What's that? I'll say no more of it,   3555
Who have nothing left to say.
I've asked a stupid question.
That which I had in my hands
Was the greatest joy of all,
But I couldn't keep it. And he   3560
Who loses such joy, and loses it
For good cause, has no right to happiness."

And while he moaned and ranted
A miserable prisoner, a woman

Who'd been shut in that chapel, saw him,   3565
And heard every word he said,
Through the cracks in the wall. And as soon
As his fainting spell had ended
She called out loud: "Lord!
Who do I hear out there?   3570
Who is it, complaining like that?"
And he answered: "And who are you?"
"I am a prisoner," she answered,
"The most miserable person alive."
And he answered: "Be quiet, you idiot!   3575
Compared to what I am suffering
Your sadness is joy, your evil
Is good. The more a man
Is accustomed to a happy life,
The more he's distracted and bewildered   3580
By sorrow, if it comes to him. Even
A feeble man can carry
A burden, simply from habit,
That someone of infinitely greater
Strength can't manage at all."   3585
"Indeed!" she said. "I quite
Understand how truly you've spoken,
But I hardly believe it gives you
The right to say your misfortune
Is greater than mine. And it's not.   3590
For you, I believe, can go
Wherever you like, and I
Am imprisoned in here, and fate
Has so arranged it that tomorrow
They'll come to this place and take me   3595
Away, under sentence of death."
"My God!" said he. "For what crime?"
"Good knight! May God deny me
Eternal mercy for my soul

If in any way I've deserved this!   3600
But I'll tell you the simple truth,
Without a lying word,
As to why I'm here in this prison.
I've been accused of treason,
And there's no one I can find to defend me,   3605
To keep me from the stake or the gallows."
"Well," he went on, "in the first place,
Plainly my sorrow and my pain
Are greater than yours, for there could be
Someone, could there not, who could come   3610
And save you from this danger. Isn't that
True?" "Yes. But who?
There's no one I know who would do it.
There are only two men in all
The world who would dare to defend me   3615
By fighting three men at once."
"What? My God, against three?"
"Yes, my lord, I assure you.
There are three who accuse me of treason."
"And who are those, who love you   3620
So much, that either of them
Might be brave enough to fight
Against three in order to save you?"
"I'll tell you the simple truth:
One is my lord Gawain,   3625
The other is my lord Yvain—
And Yvain is the reason I'll be wrongly
Brought to martyrdom and to death."
"For whom?" he exclaimed. "For whom?"
"My lord! So help me God,   3630
Because of King Urien's son."
"Now I understand! But if
You die, he'll die too.
For I am that same Yvain

Because of whom you live   3635
In such terror. And you, I think,
Are the girl who kept me in that room,
Who protected me, who saved my life
And my body when I was trapped
Between the two gates, when I   3640
Was troubled and miserable, when I
Was worried and desperate and unsure.
And I'd have been killed or captured,
If you hadn't helped me. Now tell me,
My sweet good friend! Who   3645
Has accused you of treason and had you
Shut away in this dungeon?"
"My lord! I'll hide nothing from you,
Not when you've asked me to speak.
It's true: I was hardly halfhearted,   3650
I helped you loyally when you needed it.
It was my advice that led
My lady to receive you; she listened
To me, she believed what I said.
And by the holy Rosary   3655
I did it more for her good
Than yours. That's what I thought—
And I still think. I admit it: I worked
For her honor, and your desire,
So help me God! But when   3660
It turned out that you were staying
Away longer than a year,
And you ought to be back with my lady
But weren't, she grew angry with me,
Thinking she'd been betrayed   3665
By following my advice.
And as soon as her steward found out,
He saw his chance to stir up
Trouble between her and me—

A dishonest, thieving scoundrel   3670
Who'd always been jealous of me,
Because my lady believed me,
And trusted me, more than him.
In her court, in front of everyone,
He accused me of treachery on your   3675
Behalf. And there was no one to help me
Except myself, though I knew
I'd never betrayed my lady,
Not in deed or in word. Never!
I was horrified, and I answered—not bothering   3680
To consult with anyone—that I'd
Be defended by a single knight,
Who would fight with three accusers
At once. And he hadn't the courtesy
To deny my offer. I'd said it,   3685
And he wouldn't let me withdraw it
Or take it back, no matter
What. So they took me at my word,
And I had only forty
Days to find a knight   3690
Willing and able to fight
Against three at once. I was pledged,
It was done. I've been to many
Courts, including King Arthur's,
But no one could help me, and no one   3695
Could give me any useful word
Of you, for they had no news."
"But tell me: my lord Gawain,
So gracious, so good, where was he?
No helpless girl has ever   3700
Come to him for help
And found him unwilling to give it."
"Had I found him at court, I know
That nothing I asked for would ever

Have been denied me. But some knight   3705
Had stolen away the queen,
Or so they told me. And surely
The king was out of his mind
To let her go anywhere near him.
It was Kay, I think, who took her   3710
To meet the knight who carried
Her off, which disturbed my lord
Gawain so much that he's gone
To find her. And he'll never come back
Until he's found her, he'll never   3715
Rest. And there's the whole truth,
I've told you everything that happened.
Tomorrow, I'm sure to die
A contemptible death, burned
At the stake for the wrongs you've committed!"   3720
And he answered: "God forbid
That anyone hurt you on my
Account! While I'm alive
You're safe! Expect me tomorrow,
Ready to do what I can,   3725
Offering my body for your freedom,
As indeed I ought to do.
But be careful, tell no one here
Who I am—no one! However
The battle goes, make sure   3730
That no one knows my name!"
"Of course, my lord! No one
Could torture it out of me.
I'd rather they killed me first,
Since you wish no one to know you.   3735
But I beg you, all the same,
Not to return simply
For me. I've no desire
To see you in so dangerous a battle.

I thank you for your promise of help,   3740
Given so willingly, but consider
Yourself released from all burdens.
Better that I die, only I,
Than to see them rejoicing first
At your death, and then at mine—   3745
For they'd never let me go,
Once you'd been killed. It's better
That you remain alive
Than they kill the two of us at once."
"Now that is very insulting,   3750
My friend!" answered Yvain.
"Perhaps you really don't wish
Deliverance from death, or else
You look down at the sort of assistance
I've offered to give you. I refuse   3755
To discuss it any longer. With all
You've done for me, it's utterly
Impossible that I fail to help you
No matter what you may need.
I understand that you're very frightened,   3760
But with God's good help, and I trust
In Him, I'll dishonor the three of them.
That's enough of that: I'm off
To find some lodging in this wood,
For there's nothing available here."   3765
"My lord!" she answered. "May God
Give you good shelter, and good night,
And keep you, as I pray He will,
Safe from anything that might harm you!"
So Yvain left her, and the lion,   3770
As usual, followed behind him,
And they went along till they came
To a baron's stronghold, a castle
Completely enclosed by a thick

Stone wall, tall and well built.   3775
No catapult, no stone-throwing machine,
Could hope to attack that castle,
Built and fortified as it was,
And yet outside its walls
The earth had been levelled so flat   3780
That neither house nor hut
Remained. You'll learn the reason
Later, when it's time to know it.
My lord Yvain came straight
Toward the castle, taking the road   3785
As it led him, and seven servants
Came out to meet him, and let
The drawbridge down. But as soon
As they saw the lion who was with him
They were terribly frightened, and asked   3790
Yvain, if it pleased him, to leave
The lion at the gate, so he couldn't
Hurt them or kill them. And he answered:
"Say no more! If he can't
Come in, neither can I.   3795
Either receive us both
Or I remain out here:
I love him as I love myself.
And yet, there's nothing to fear!
I'll watch him so carefully that you'll all   3800
Be perfectly safe." And they answered:
"May it be as you say!" And so
They entered that walled town,
And went until they met
Knights and ladies and pretty   3805
Young girls coming toward them,
Greeting Yvain, ready
To help him dismount and take off
His armor. And they said: "Welcome,

Good knight! Welcome among us!   3810
And may God grant it that you stay
Until you're able to leave
Happy and full of honor!"
From the highest down to the lowest
They welcomed him, and put themselves out   3815
To lead him joyously to the castle.
And then, expressing their joy,
They fell into a fit
Of sadness, and forgot their happiness,
And began to moan and cry   3820
And weep and tear at themselves.
And on and on they went,
One moment happy, then weeping,
Welcoming their guest happily
But somehow not seeming to mean it,   3825
For indeed there was something frightening them,
Something that would happen tomorrow,
They were sure, they were certain, and they thought
It would come by noontime. And my lord
Yvain was bewildered, seeing them   3830
Constantly changing from sadness
To joy, and from joy to sadness,
So he spoke to the lord of the castle
And asked him, please, to explain.
"Good God, dear sir!" he exclaimed,   3835
"I beg you, tell me why
I've been welcomed with so much honor,
Such joy, and so much weeping?"
"Yes, if you wish to know.
But you'd do better to forget   3840
You asked, to prefer silence.
And I prefer not to tell you
Anything to make you unhappy.
Just let us grieve as we must,

And pay no attention." "Impossible,"   3845
Yvain answered. "I could never
See you struck by such sadness
And not feel it in my heart, too.
And so I ask you again,
No matter what sadness it might bring me."   3850
"Well then," was the answer, "I'll tell you.
I've been deeply afflicted by a giant.
He wants me to give him my daughter,
Whose beauty surpasses that
Of any girl in the world.   3855
And the name of this monster, may God
Destroy him, is Harpin of the Mountain.
And every day he steals
Anything of mine he can get at.
No one has a better right   3860
Than I to complain and be sorrowful.
I may lose my mind from grief,
For I had six sons, all knights,
Handsomer than any in the world,
And this giant has captured them all.   3865
He killed two while I watched,
And tomorrow he'll kill the others
Unless I can find someone
To fight him for their freedom, or else
Hand over my daughter—and he says   3870
That, once he has her, he intends
To give her to the vilest, the filthiest
Knaves he can find in his household,
For their entertainment. He
Himself wouldn't stoop so low.   3875
And this is the grief I wait for,
Tomorrow, if God does not help me.
It's hardly remarkable, my dear
Good sir, if all of us weep.

But for your sake, and politeness, we're trying   3880
As best we can for a moment
Or two of laughter and delight:
Anyone who invites a true gentleman
To visit, and fails to honor him,
Is a fool, and you strike me as noble   3885
Indeed. Now you've heard everything,
The entire story of our sorrow.
The giant has left us nothing,
Neither in this castle nor the town
Around it, except what you see.   3890
You may have noticed, yourself,
As you came here this evening, how he's left us
Nothing that might be worth
An egg, except these walls—
And they're new, for he levelled the town.   3895
When he'd stolen everything he wanted,
He set fire to the rest. And these
Are the evil things he's done to me."

My lord Yvain listened
To everything his host told him,   3900
And when he'd heard him out
He was happy to answer him: "Sir!"
He said. "Your troubles distress me,
And make me exceedingly angry,
But one thing I find astonishing: 3905
Tell me, why haven't you sought
For help at King Arthur's court?
No one, no matter how mighty,
Could come to that court and not find
Someone willing to test   3910
Their prowess against his." And then

That wealthy baron explained
That yes, he'd surely have had
The help he needed, if only
He'd known where to find Sir Gawain.   3915
"He'd never have taken it lightly,
For my wife is his sister by blood.
But a knight from some strange country,
Who came to that court seeking her,
Has taken the king's wife.   3920
He could never have led her away,
To be sure, entirely by himself.
It was Kay, who so befuddled
The king that he allowed the queen
To pass under his protection.   3925
The king was a fool, and the queen
Reckless, entrusting herself
To Kay. But I am the one
Who truly suffers, and loses,
For who can doubt that my lord   3930
Gawain, that noble knight,
Would have hurried here as fast
As he could, had he known this was happening,
Would have saved his niece and his nephews.
But he knows nothing, which hurts me   3935
So deeply that my heart is half broken.
Gawain has gone off hunting
The villain who stole the queen—
May God bring him sorrow and shame!"
Sigh after sigh came   3940
From Yvain, hearing these words.
Pity worked in him and made him
Answer: "My dear good sir!
I'll be glad to take on this adventure,
And its dangers, if only the giant   3945
And your sons come here tomorrow

Early enough not
To cause me too much delay,
Because by noon tomorrow
I must be somewhere else,   3950
As I've given my word to be."
"Good sir!" exclaimed the baron,
"I thank you a thousand times,
And more, for your willingness to help."
And all the folk of his household   3955
Spoke exactly as he had.

And then his daughter came
From an inside room, graceful
And beautiful and pleasing, and exceedingly
Modest, sad, and silent.   3960
Her sorrows knew no limit;
She walked with her head bent low,
And her mother walked beside her,
Showing their obedience to their lord,
The host of that house, who'd sent for them.   3965
They came with their mantles wrapped
Around them, to cover their tears,
And he ordered them to open their mantles
And raise their heads, saying:
"You shouldn't be upset because   3970
I've asked you to come out. God
And good luck have brought us a kind
And noble knight, of wonderfully
Good birth, who promises me
He'll fight the giant. Don't wait   3975
Another moment, don't
Delay: throw yourselves
At his feet!" "God keep me from any

Such sight!" said Yvain at once.
"Now, it would hardly be right   3980
For my lord Gawain's sister
To throw herself at my feet,
Nor his niece. May God protect me
From ever feeling such pride
That I let them lie at my feet!   3985
Please: I could never forget
My shame, if I ever permitted it.
But surely they can allow
Themselves to be pleased and comforted,
At least till tomorrow, when they'll know   3990
If God wishes them to be helped.
I've no need to ask for anything
Else, except that the giant
Come soon, so I won't break my promise.
For I can't permit anything   3995
To keep me, tomorrow at noon,
From the greatest undertaking, truly,
That I could ever attempt."
And so he kept himself
From promising too much, worried   4000
That in fact the giant might not
Come in time to let him
Reach the girl locked
In the chapel and be able to help her.
Still, what he promised was enough   4005
To make them feel hopeful, and everyone
Offered him thanks, trusting
In his prowess, sure of his strength,
Believing he must be a hero
If he shares his journey with a lion   4010
Who goes along beside him
As sweetly as any lamb.
And the hope he'd brought them gave them

Such comfort, made them so happy,
That they completely forgot their sorrow.   4015
When the hour struck, he was led
To sleep in a brightly lit room,
Escorted to his bed by both
The girl and her mother, for he
Was already dear to them both,   4020
And would have been a hundred
Thousand times more had they truly
Known his courtesy and the battles
He had won. And he and the lion
Lay down together, and slept.   4025
No one was brave enough
To sleep with them: indeed, they closed
The door of the room so tightly
That they couldn't come out until morning.
And then, when they'd unlocked the door,   4030
He rose and heard Mass—and waited.
And because of his promise he waited
Until the hour of prime,
Then called them all together,
Including his host, and said: 4035
"My lord! There's no more time.
I need to go, with your leave;
I can't allow myself
To linger. Believe me, for it's true,
That I'd gladly, I'd cheerfully wait   4040
Even longer, for the sake of Sir Gawain's
Nephews, and his niece, for I love him
Dearly, except that the business
Awaiting me is desperately urgent,
And I've very far to go!"   4045
And then the girl's mind
Quivered and reeled with fear,
And her mother's, and her father's too.

They were so afraid that he'd leave
That they thought of throwing themselves   4050
Full length at his feet, until
They remembered his words and realized
He'd think it neither good nor proper.
Then the baron offered to give him
Anything he owned, land   4055
Or anything else, whatever
He wanted, if only he'd wait
A bit longer. And he answered: "May God
Protect me from accepting anything
From you!" And the terrified girl   4060
Began to weep and moan,
Begging him to stay. Utterly
Anguished, totally distraught,
She begged him by the glorious queen
Of Heaven, and the angels on high,   4065
And by God Himself, not to go,
But to wait a little longer.
And she begged him by her uncle, who he says
He knows and loves and thinks well of.
And an infinite pity seized him,   4070
Hearing her call on him in the name
Of the man he loved best in the world,
And by the mother of Heaven,
And in God's own name, to him
The honey and sweetness of pity.   4075
And anguish filled him, and he sighed,
For not by his father's kingdom
Could he see her burned at the stake,
That girl ·he'd promised to help.
He'd either go out of his mind,   4080
Or cut his life short, if he couldn't
Reach her in time. And yet,
On the other hand, it pained him

Even to think of the kindness
Of Gawain, his friend. And his heart   4085
Came close to splitting in his body,
Knowing he could not wait.
And yet he waited, not moving,
And lingered, and stayed there longer,
Till the giant came pounding up,   4090
Leading along the knights
He'd captured. A club hung from
His neck, huge and sharpened,
And he used it to prod them along.
And the knights were dressed in clothing   4095
Worth less than a straw, only
Dirty, stinking shirts.
And he'd tied them tight, ropes
On their feet and hands, and mounted them
On four stumping packhorses,   4100
Swaybacked, and skinny, and feeble.
These horses came riding along
A wood, and a dwarf, puffed
Like an ox, had tied their tails
Together, and walking beside them   4105
Beat them as he went, with a lash
With four knots, plainly impressed
With himself and feeling most brave;
Indeed, he beat them till they bled.
And so the giant and the dwarf   4110
Led those knights, to their shame.
Stopping in front of the gate,
In the middle of the plain, the giant
Shouted to the baron that he'd kill
His sons, unless he handed   4115
Over his daughter—and her
He'd give to his scum, as a slut,
For he himself no longer

Cared for her or would bother to take her.
She'd have a thousand of the scum   4120
All over her, all the time,
Filthy, naked scum,
Kitchen slaves and stablemen,
All of them wanting their share.
And the baron was almost out of   4125
His mind, hearing how they'd use
His daughter as a whore, if they got her,
And if they didn't they'd kill
His four sons in front of his eyes.
He suffered like someone who'd rather   4130
Be dead than alive, exclaiming
"Oh God, I'm miserable!" and weeping
Bitter tears, and sighing.
And then my good and gentle
Lord Yvain spoke to him: 4135
"Sir! He's cruel and presumptuous,
This giant, swaggering out there.
But God will not suffer him
To have your daughter in his power!
He's full of contempt for her, he'd love   4140
To shame her, but it would be tragic
For such a beautiful creature,
Born of such noble parents,
To be handed over to scullions.
My weapons, hurry! and my horse!   4145
Let down the drawbridge, so I
Can ride out there! One
Of us must fall, he
Or I, I know not which.
If I can humble that savage   4150
Beast, that cruel villain,
Who's been abusing you,
And make him surrender your sons,

And then apologize
For the shameful words he's spoken,   4155
I'd gladly commend you to God
And go about my business."
And so they fetched him his horse,
And brought him his weapons, and worked
To get him well armored, quickly   4160
Equipped for battle, getting him
Ready as fast as their hands
Could move, without wasting a moment.
And when he was armored and ready
There was nothing left but to lower   4165
The drawbridge and let him ride out.
They lowered it, and out he went—
But the lion had no intention
Of staying behind. All those
Who remained in the castle commended   4170
Yvain to their Lord's keeping,
Terribly afraid that the fiend,
The demon, who'd already killed
So many good knights in front
Of their eyes, in that very same place,   4175
Might be able to do it again.
They prayed to God to keep death
From Yvain, to return him alive
And well, and to let him kill
The giant. So all of them fervently   4180
Prayed to God for what all of them
Wished. And the giant approached him
Fiercely, and threatened him, saying:
"By my eyes, whoever sent you
Out here isn't much of a friend!   4185
But he couldn't have planned a better
Way for getting revenge.
Whatever you did to him, or meant to,

He'll have a perfect revenge."
But Yvain, who felt no fear,   4190
Answered: "What a lot of noise!
Do your best, and I'll
Do mine. Stupid words
Bore me." And Yvain charged him,
Worried that he might be late.   4195
And he aimed his lance at his chest,
Protected behind a bearskin.
And the giant came running at him,
Beating at Yvain with his club.
And Yvain struck so hard   4200
At his chest that he pierced the skin,
Then having no sauce, dipped
The tip of his lance in blood.
And the giant beat him with his club
Till the knight bent to escape him.   4205
Then Yvain drew the sword
He knew how to swing so well,
And finding the giant unprotected,
Trusting so much in his strength
That he scorned the use of armor,   4210
Went at him with the sharp blade
And slashed him so well, not bothering
With the flat side, cut him
So fiercely, that he sliced a piece
The size of a steak from his cheek.   4215
And the giant him so hard
In return that he bent his head
Down to the horse's neck.
And the lion bristled at this blow,
Ready to help his master,   4220
Then leaped angrily, powerfully,
And seized the giant's bearskin
And ripped and tore it like bark,

And bit out of his hide
A chunk of his hip, tore it   4225
Meat and muscle alike.
And the giant ran, roaring
And bellowing like a bull, for the lion
Had hurt him badly. He lifted
His club with both hands, and tried   4230
To strike the lion, but missed,
For the lion jumped back, and the giant
Wasted his blow. It hit
The ground, useless, near
Yvain, touching neither lion   4235
Nor man. And quickly Yvain
Swung at him, and again, and hit him,
And before the giant knew
What was happening the sword had severed
His shoulder from his body. And the very   4240
Next blow ran the length
Of the sword just under his chest,
Straight into the liver. And the giant
Fell, death reaching out
To take him. I doubt that a giant   4245
Oak crashing down
Could topple with a louder sound.
And all those standing on the walls
Had been waiting to see that blow.
And they learned which of them ran fastest,   4250
For they all came running after
The spoils, like dogs at a hunt,
Who chase the fox till they catch him.
Everyone tried to get
To the giant first, there   4255
Where he lay on his face; no one
Held back. And the baron ran,
And everyone in his court ran,

And his daughter ran, and his wife.
And the four brothers, who had suffered   4260
So much, were happy. And everyone
Knew there was nothing they could do
To keep my lord Yvain
There, it was perfectly clear,
But all the same they begged him   4265
To come back, to celebrate, as soon
As he'd done whatever business
He was going off to do.
And he answered that he wouldn't dare
To promise a thing, for how   4270
It might go with him, for good
Or for ill, he could not say.
But he told his host this much:
He and his sons and his daughter
Ought to take the dwarf and go   4275
To my lord Gawain, as soon
As they've heard that Gawain is home,
And tell him the entire tale,
Let him know what was done.
For what use is kindness, if it's kept   4280
In the dark? It needs to be known.
And they said: "It shouldn't be hidden,
This kindness. That wouldn't be right.
We'll do exactly exactly as you wish.
But tell us, so we can tell him   4285
When we stand in front of him, what
We can say? How can we praise you,
When none of us know your name?"
And he answered: "Tell him this much,
When you stand in front of him. Tell him   4290
That I told you my name was the Knight
Of the Lion. And tell him, too,
I beg you, that I have asked you

To say that he knows me well,
As I know him, even   4295
If he doesn't know he knows.
And say nothing more, I beg you.
And now I'm obliged to leave you,
And nothing worries me more
Than that I may have waited too long,   4300
For surely before it turns noon
I'll have more than enough to do,
If indeed I can get there in time."
He started, unwilling to delay.
And his host begged him to accept   4305
The handsomest gift he could make,
And take his four sons with him.
Every one of them would try
To serve him, if only he'd let them.
But wanting no one to ride   4310
With him, Yvain left them
Standing where they were, and went off.
And immediately he headed his horse
Straight toward the chapel, spurring him
As fast as he could. The road   4315
Was both good and straight, and he knew
How to keep to the road. But before
He could get to the chapel, they'd dragged out
The girl and gotten the pyre
Ready, piled up the wood   4320
Where they meant to burn her. Totally
Naked, except for her shift,
They had her tied where the fire
Was lit, accused of a crime
That had never crossed her mind.   4325
And then Yvain arrived,
And saw her near the fire, where they'd thrown her,
And his anger flared, as it should have:

Anyone who doubts that knows nothing
Of courtesy, and is devoid of wisdom.   4330
He was very, very angry,
But also perfectly confident
That God and justice would help him,
Would fight at his side. He put
His trust completely in such comrades,   4335
Though he never forgot the lion.
Galloping straight at the crowd
He came, shouting: "Release her!
Release her, you evil people!
There's no justice in burning someone   4340
At the stake who's done nothing—nothing!"
And they all pulled back, and made way,
And let him approach. And yet
What he really wanted to see
For himself was she whom his heart   4345
Saw everywhere, wherever she might be.
And he looked until he found her,
And forced his heart to meet
The challenge, held it back, held it in,
As one struggles, finding the strength   4350
To curb a bucking horse.
And still he stared at her eagerly,
Sighing as he watched, but not sighing
Quite so hard as he might have,
So no one would know who he was.   4355
It was hard, but he stifled his pain.
And an immense pity seized him,
Hearing and seeing and understanding
The poor ladies of that court,
Who were moaning and weeping and crying,   4360
"Oh God! You've forgotten us!
We'll be left here hopeless, lost,
If we lose so good a friend,

So good an adviser, and a helper,
So useful for all of us at court!   4365
It was her advice that led
Our lady to give us fine
New dresses. It will all be different,
There'll be no one left to speak for us.
Curses on whoever takes her   4370
Away! Curses for our loss!
It's going to be awful for us!
There'll be no one to say and suggest:
'This ermine cloak, this coat,
And this coat, too, my lady,   4375
That worthy woman should have them!
Indeed, what a wonderful thing
It would be to send them to her,
For she needs them so badly, she does.'
Who else will say such things?   4380
There's no one as generous, as courteous.
Everyone else is always
Asking for herself and not
For others, though they really need nothing."

And so they were carrying on,   4385
And Yvain, standing among them
And hearing all their complaints,
Knew they were true, not invented.
And seeing Lunette on her knees,
Stripped down to her shift,   4390
Having made her confession and begged
The Lord to forgive her for her sins,
Make her innocent of all guilt,
He who had loved her so dearly

Came toward her, and lifted her up,   4395
And said: "Oh girl! Where
Are those who reproach you, who accuse you?
Here and now, unless
They refuse it, I offer them battle."
And she, who had not noticed him,   4400
Who had not looked up as he came,
Replied: "Lord! You come
From God, in my hour of need!
Those who've sworn false witness
Are standing here all around me.   4405
Had you come just a little later
They'd have burned me to charcoal and cinders.
And here you are to defend me:
May God give you the power
To succeed in exactly the measure   4410
That I stand innocent of their charges!"
The steward, and the steward's two brothers,
Heard these words. "Ha!"
They cried. "You creature, miser
Of truth and spendthrift of lies!   4415
He'd have to be crazy to take on
Such a burden for anything you'd said.
And he must be a numbskull, this knight
Who's come here to die for you.
There's only one of him   4420
And three of us. I advise him
To run before it's too late."
And Yvain answered, furious:
"Let anyone run who's afraid!
I'm not so worried by three shields   4425
That I'd run from a fight without fighting.
What sort of knight would I be
If I let you hold this field
While I stood healthy and unharmed?"

As long as I'm alive and well   4430
I'll never run from your threats.
Let me advise you. Pronounce
This girl, against whom you've hurled
Such slanders, innocent of everything—
For she tells me, and I believe her,   4435
And she swears to me on her faith
And upon her immortal soul
That she's never betrayed her lady
In word, or in deed, or in thought.
I believe every word she's spoken,   4440
And I will defend her, if I can.
I believe in the justice of her cause.
And let this truth be known:
Those who stand for justice
Stand with God, who is justice   4445
And right. And with them at my side
I fight with better comrades
Beside me than any of you."
Then the steward answered, stupidly,
That he'd do what he could to oblige him   4450
In everything, to his heart's content,
If the lion would leave him alone.
And Yvain answered that he hadn't
Brought the lion as his champion,
And he needed no one's help,   4455
But if the lion chose to attack him
He'd better defend himself;
He could guarantee nothing. And the steward
Answered: "Your words mean nothing.
Unless you curb your lion   4460
And make him stand aside,
You'd better not linger here,
But leave! It would show good sense,
For everyone here in this country

Knows she's betrayed her lady,   4465
And it's right and just that she have
Her reward in flame and fire."
"The Holy Spirit prevent it!"
Cried Yvain, who knew the truth.
"May God keep me here   4470
Until I've set her free!"
And he ordered the lion to withdraw,
And stay still, and the lion did
Exactly as his master asked.

The lion was safely to one side,   4475
And all the talking between them
Was done, and they got ready to charge.
The three of them pointed their spears,
But he proceeded at a walk,
Determined not to try   4480
For too much at the very first blow.
He let them splinter their lances,
Keeping his own intact,
Letting them use his shield
As a target. And all of them broke   4485
Their spears. And then he rode off,
An acre or more distant,
Not planning to stay there long.
Galloping straight at the steward   4490
He reached him first, and smashed him
So hard with his lance that he knocked him
To the ground, no matter what he did,
And gave him so stunning a blow
That for a long time he lay there   4495
In a daze, unable to bother him.
Then the other two attacked him,

Swords in their hands, and both
Landed good blows, but got
Better ones back. Each   4500
Of his blows was easily worth
Two of theirs. And so
He defended himself so well
There was no advantage in numbers,
Until at last the steward   4505
Rose and did what he could
To hurt him, and the others tried too,
Until they began to beat him.
And the lion, watching all this,
Thought it was time to help,   4510
For his master seemed to need it.
And the ladies, all in one voice,
Deeply devoted to the girl,
Called on God to help him
And prayed with all their hearts   4515
That nothing might bring defeat
Or injury or death to him
Who fought that battle for their friend.
Having no other weapons,
The ladies helped with their prayers.   4520
And the lion brought him different
Assistance, leaping so fiercely
At the steward, who was fighting on foot,
Attacking so furiously that he scattered
The mail from his armor like so much   4525
Straw, and seizing him in his jaws
Dragged him down so viciously
That he ripped the flesh from his shoulder
All along his side.
Whatever he bit at he stripped   4530
Away, till the guts hung out.
But the other two paid him back.

And now the battle was even.
The steward lay dying, death
At his throat, writhing and rolling   4535
In the waves of warm red blood
Flowing out of his body.
And the lion attacked the others—
For nothing Yvain could do
Could drive him off, though he hit him   4540
And threatened him and struggled to do all
He could. Somehow the lion
Seemed to know that his master
Did not truly dislike
His help, but loved him better   4545
For it. He charged against them
Until they had reason to complain,
And slashed him with their weapons, and hurt him.
And seeing his lion wounded
My lord Yvain was angry,   4550
And with reason, and he took such savage
Revenge, attacking with such stunning
Blows that he wore them down,
Reduced them to feeble nothingness.
And unable to defend themselves   4555
They surrendered, crying for mercy.
The lion's assistance had beaten them,
But the lion was badly hurt,
Wounded all over his body,
With good reason for pain and fear.   4560
And my lord Yvain himself
Was hardly in the best of health,
His body cut and slashed.
But he worried less for himself

Than for his suffering lion.   4565
Now he'd freed the girl,
Exactly as he meant to, and the lady
Had pardoned her servant, completely
And cheerfully. And the fire lit
For Lunette has burned those   4570
Who lit it, intending it for her,
For justice requires that he
Who has wrongly condemned another
Should die precisely the death
He'd meant for a different victim.   4575
And Lunette was smiling, happy
To be at one with her mistress,
Both of them filled with a joy
Greater than anyone had ever
Felt. And everyone pledged   4580
Eternal service to Yvain,
Though no one knew who he was,
Not even the lady, who already
Had his heart without knowing it.
And she begged him to stay there for as long   4585
As it took for both lion and man
To rest and recover. And he said:
"Lady! It's out of the question.
I could not stay here unless
My mistress pardoned me, forgave me,   4590
And forgot her anger and displeasure.
And that would end my affliction."
"Ah," she said, "that upsets me.
Anyone who thinks ill of you
Can't be a courteous woman.   4595
She couldn't shut her door
On a knight as worthy as you
Unless he'd done her some terrible
Wrong." "Lady! However

It hurts, it pleases me, if it's what   4600
She wants. But no more of that!
I'll say nothing of the offense, and nothing
Of the punishment, except to those
Who already know the whole story."
"Does anyone know it, other than   4605
You two?" "Oh yes, lady!"
"But tell us your name, good sir!
Tell us that much, at least!
And then you're discharged, you can go."
"Discharged, lady? Oh no.   4610
I owe more than I could pay.
But I owe you at least my name.
If anyone speaks of the Knight
Of the Lion they're speaking of me.
And that is the name I've chosen."   4615
"Before God, good sir! We've never
Seen you, we've never heard
That name. What does this mean?"
"Lady! I suppose you ought
To conclude that I'm not really   4620
Well known." And the lady replied:
"Still, if it wouldn't displease you,
I'd like to ask you to stay."
"My lady! How could I dare,
Not knowing for certain if I'd won   4625
My mistress' goodwill again?"
"Then go with God, good sir!
And if it's God's will, may he turn
Your sorrow and suffering to joy!"
"Lady! I pray that He hears you!"   4630
Then he whispered, under his breath:
"Oh lady! you don't know it, but my happiness
Is locked away in a chest,
And you carry the key, only you."

And then, suffering immensely,   4635
He left. And the only one
Who knew him was Lunette, who rode
A long way at his side. Only
Lunette went with him, and he begged her
Over and over not   4640
To let anyone know who
Her champion had been. "My lord!"
She said. "I'll never tell."
And then he went on, and asked her
Not to forget him, and to keep   4645
A place for him in his lady's heart
If she had the chance. And she told him
Not to worry. She could never
Forget him, nor ever be unfaithful
Or stop trying to help. And he thanked her   4650
A thousand times. And he left her,
Worried and sad on account
Of his lion, who had to be carried,
For he couldn't have followed on foot.
He'd filled his shield with ferns   4655
And moss, and made it a litter,
The softest bed he could manage,
And laid the lion gently
Down, and carried him, lying
Full length on the inside of the shield.   4660
And so his horse bore him
Away, and he came to the door
Of a handsome house, a strong house.
The gate was closed, so he called,
And the porter opened it for him   4665
So swiftly that he never needed

To say another word.
And he held out his hand for the reins,
Saying: "Good sir, come in!
My lord's house is open to you,   4670
Should you care to dismount." And Yvain
Answered: "I'm pleased to accept,
For this is something I very much
Need, this offer of shelter."

And so he went through the door   4675
And saw all the people
Of that household coming to help him.
They greeted him, and helped him dismount,
And laid down his shield, with the lion
On it, on a stone bench.   4680
And some of them took his horse
And brought it to a stable, and others
Took his weapons and his armor,
Exactly as they ought to. And then
The lord of that house heard   4685
That he'd come, and as soon as he knew it
Hurried to the courtyard to greet him.
And his wife hurried after him,
And all her sons and daughters,
And many others, a crowd   4690
Of all sorts, happy to welcome him.
And they put him in a quiet room,
Seeing how sick he seemed,
And behaved equally well
By putting his lion in with him.   4695
And two young girls, daughters
Of the master of the house, both of them
Wonderfully skilled in medicine,

Were put in charge of his cure.
How many days did he stay there?   4700
I don't know, but until he
And his lion were cured and could leave.

But during this time it happened
That the Lord of Blackthorn was so fiercely   4705
Attacked by Death that it forced him
To yield, and he died. And dying
He left two daughters, and after
His death the older of the two
Said that everything he had owned   4710
On earth was hers, free
And clear, to have and to hold
For life, and nothing belonged
To her sister. And her sister said
She'd go to King Arthur's court,   4715
Seeking someone to help her
Defend her rights. And the older
Sister, seeing she couldn't
Prevail without a struggle,
Was terribly worried and decided   4720
That if she could she'd get
To Arthur's court before her.
So she got herself dressed and ready
And neither delayed nor waited,
But hurried off to court.   4725
And the younger sister followed
As fast as she could, but her journey
Got her nowhere, for her older
Sister had already argued
Her case to my lord Gawain,   4730
And he had bound himself

To do as she wished. But they
Had also agreed that should she
Tell anyone else what had happened
He would never defend her again,   4735
And she had sworn to those terms.

And then the younger sister
Arrived, wearing a short
Woolen gown, trimmed
With fresh ermine. It was just three days   4740
Since the queen had come back from imprisonment,
Stolen by Melegant and held
Along with his other prisoners;
Only Lancelot had been left
Behind, treacherously locked   4745
In a tower. And the day the younger
Sister came to court
Was the very same day they heard
The news of the cruel, evil
Giant, killed in battle   4750
By the Knight of the Lion, at whose
Directions and in whose name
His nephews had greeted Gawain,
Telling him the great service
Done them by that knight, and his great   4755
Bravery. And his niece told him
Everything, explaining that he knew
This knight well, though not his name.

And the younger sister heard

All this talk, which left her anxious   4760
And worried, desperate, bewildered—
Thinking to herself, what sort
Of help could she find at court
If all the best knights were away?
And more than once she'd approached   4765
My lord Gawain, begging him
For love and for charity to help her.
And he'd said: "My friend! You're wasting
Your time. There's nothing I can do.
I've taken on something else,   4770
And I'm not about to leave it."
And she left him as quickly as she could
And came directly to the king.
"Your Majesty!" she said. "I've come
To you and your court seeking   4775
Help. I've found none. I'm astonished
That no one here will help me.
And yet I'd be acting improperly
If I left without your permission.
For my sister might have known   4780
That love could have gotten her whatever
She wanted, anything I owned,
But force will never make me
Abandon my inheritance, never—
If only I can find assistance!"   4785
"You've spoken wisely," said the king.
"And while she's here, I advise her,
And I beg her, to let you have
What is rightly yours." But the older
Sister, sure of having   4790
The very best knight in the world,
Answered: "My lord! May God
Blast me if I'll give her anything
I own, a castle or a town

Or a forest, or a square of burned land,   4795
Not even a tree! And if there's
A knight who'll defend her, though I doubt it,
Anyone who'll support her right,
Let him come forward, and now!"
"Your offer is distinctly improper,"   4800
Said the king. "More time is required.
According to the judgment of all
Our courts, she can take as long
As forty days to find
A champion." And she answered: "Your Majesty!   4805
You have the right to proclaim
The law as it pleases you, and seems right.
And it's not for me to tell you
Your right seems wrong. I have
No choice. I consent to a delay,   4810
If she demands one." And the younger
Sister said she definitely
Wanted a delay. And then
She commended the king to God
And left his court, determined   4815
To hunt all over the world
For the rest of her life
For the Knight of the Lion, he
Who strove to help a woman
Anywhere who truly needed it.   4820

And so she began her quest,
And travelled through many countries,
But heard nothing of him,
Which caused her such pain that she sickened
And grew ill. Yet that was lucky,   4825
For it brought her to a friend's house,

Where she was dearly loved, and they saw
At once, looking at her face,
That her health was not very good.
And they made her stay, against   4830
Her will, till she'd told them everything.
And then another young woman
Took on the journey she'd begun,
Carrying on her quest.
And so while one woman rested   4835
The other rode the whole day
Long, rode fast, rode alone,
Until the darkness of night
Fell, and she was frightened.
And then frightened still more   4840
When it rained as hard as God
Could make it rain, and she
Was deep in the forest. And the night
And the forest worried her, but worse
Than either the forest or the night—   4845
Far worse—was the rain. And the roads
Became so foul that sometimes
Her horse was almost up
To its belly in mud, which might
Thoroughly frighten any   4850
Young woman alone in a wood,
With no escort, in such weather and on such
A night, so black that she couldn't
See the horse she sat on.
And so she prayed to God,   4855
And then she prayed to His mother,
And then to all the saints
She could think of, a litany of prayers
For God to give her shelter
And get her out of that wood.   4860
She prayed until she heard

A horn, which filled her with joy,
Sure there was shelter to be had
If only she could get to it. She headed
Toward the sound, and came   4865
To a paved road, and that road
Led her directly to the horn
She'd heard blowing in the night,
Sounding three long blasts,
Loud and high and clear.   4870
And riding straight toward the sound
She came to a cross, standing
Just to the right of the road.
And she thought that the horn and whoever
Had blown it must surely be near.   4875
So she set her horse to galloping,
And soon she came to a bridge
And saw the guardhouse and the white
Walls of a round castle.
And so, by pure chance, she got   4880
To the castle, following the sound
Of the horn, which led her along.
And that blasting horn had been blown
By a watchman mounted high
On the walls, and had caught her ear.   4885
And as soon as the watchman saw her
He hailed her, and then came down
And took the key to the gate
And opened it, and said: "Welcome,
Young woman, whoever you are!   4890
Tonight, your lodging will be good."
"Tonight, I want nothing else,"
Said the girl, as he let her in.
And after all the hardships
She'd had that day, finding   4895
Shelter was a stroke of luck,

For they looked after her well. After
She'd eaten, her host addressed her,
Asking where she was going
And what she hoped to find.   4900
And then she answered his question:
"I'm seeking someone I've never
Seen, I think, and never
Known. There's a lion with him,
And they tell me I can truly trust him,   4905
If ever I can find him." "Ah!"
He exclaimed. "I can tell you it's true—
For here in my time of great need
God sent him to me, too.
May they be blessed, whatever   4910
Paths led him to my house!
He took revenge for me on a mortal
Enemy, and made me happy
By killing him in front of my eyes.
Tomorrow, outside that gate,   4915
You can see the body of an immense
Giant, whom he killed so swiftly
That he hardly worked up a sweat."
"For God's sake, sir," cried the girl,
"Can you give me any news,   4920
Have you any idea where he went
Or where he might be staying?"
"Not a thing, as God is my witness!
But tomorrow I can put you on the road
He took when he left here." "And may God,"   4925
She answered, "take me anywhere
Where I'll truly hear where he is!
How happy I'll be, if I find him."

And so they spoke a long time
And finally went to bed.   4930
And just as soon as dawn broke
The girl arose, filled
With a deep determination
To find the man she'd been seeking.
And the master of the house rose,   4935
And all his household with him,
And they set her straight on the road
To the spring under the pine tree.
And she rode as hard as she could
Straight toward the castle town   4940
And, coming there, asked the first men
She met if they could give her
News of the knight and the lion
Who always travelled about
Together. And then they told her   4945
They had seen him fight and defeat
Three knights at once, right there
On that very same ground. And she answered
Them immediately: "Oh God!
Please: tell me everything,   4950
Now that you've told me so much.
Hide nothing, tell me what you know!"
"Nothing," they said. "We know nothing
Except what we've told you. Whatever's
Become of him we have no idea.   4955
And if she for whose sake he came here
Can't give you any news, then no one
Here possibly could.
But if you wish to ask her
Yourself, you haven't far   4960
To go, for she's come to pray
To God and hear Mass in that church,
And she's been inside so long

That her prayers must have been long ones."

And then, while they were speaking,   4965
Lunette came out of the church,
And they said: "There she is!"
And the girl went to meet her,
And they greeted each other. And the girl
Immediately asked for the news   4970
She needed, and Lunette answered
That as soon as she had a horse
Saddled and ready, she'd gladly
Ride with her and bring her
To an enclosed place where she'd left   4975
That knight. And the girl thanked her
With all her heart. The horse
Was quickly saddled and ready
And Lunette mounted at once.
And as they rode, Lunette   4980
Explained how she'd been accused
And called a traitor, and the pyre
Had been heaped and lit, and they'd meant
To put her in and burn her,
And the knight had come to help her,   4985
Just when she needed him most.
And as she spoke she led her
Along, and brought her directly
To the road where she'd left Yvain.
And having taken her so far,   4990
She said: "Follow this road
Until you come to some place
Where, if it pleases God
And the Holy Ghost, you'll hear

Truer news than I   4995
Can tell you. I remember leaving him
Right here, or very nearly
Here, but I've not seen him
Since then, and what he's done
I don't know. I know that when   5000
I left him he was wounded and needed
Help. I send you after him:
God grant that you find him healed,
If that be His will, today
Or tomorrow! Go! I commend you   5005
To God. I can follow no farther,
Or my lady might be angry."
And so they left each other,
Lunette to go home and the girl
To go on alone until   5010
She came to the house where Yvain
Had stayed and recovered his health.
She saw people in front of the gate,
Knights, and ladies, and squires,
And the lord of that house, and she greeted   5015
Them all and asked them to tell her
Anything they could, whatever
They might know, of a knight she was seeking,
A knight she needed to find.
"Who?" they asked. "He   5020
Who travels with a lion, they tell me."
"Good Lord, girl!" said the lord,
"He left us just now. You might
Be able to catch him, if you know
How to follow his tracks and you're careful   5025
Not to waste any time!"
"My lord!" she said. "God forbid!
Just tell me in what direction
I should go!" And they told her: "That way,

Right straight ahead," and they asked her   5030
To give him their greetings. But their words
Meant precious little to her.
She paid them no attention,
But immediately set off at a gallop.
To her the pace seemed terribly   5035
Slow, although her horse
Galloped very well.
And she galloped through muddy fields
Just as she galloped when the road
Was level, until she saw him,   5040
He and his lion together.
And she cried out, happily: "Help me,
Oh Lord! I finally see him,
After hunting and searching so long.
But suppose I hunt but don't win,   5045
What good will it be if I catch him?
Oh Lord, for nothing, nothing!
If I cannot get him to join me,
All my trouble will be wasted."
So saying, she hurried ahead,   5050
And her horse was dripping with sweat,
And she came where he was and greeted him.
And he answered her at once:
"God keep you, pretty one! and guard you
From worry and care!" "And the same   5055
To you, my lord, who I hope
Will be able to free me from such things!"
Then she drew her horse near his
And said: "My lord! I've sought you
All over. The fame you've earned   5060
Has led me to hunt you, all wearily,
Over many, many countries.
I've sought you so long that, God
Be thanked, I've finally found you.

And none of the misfortunes I've endured,   5065
None of the afflictions, are worth
Talking about or remembering.
It's vanished, my limbs are lightened,
Sorrow stole away
The moment I met you. Yet none   5070
Of this is my own necessity.
I come to you from a woman
Better than myself, nobler
And braver. And if you fail her,
It will be your fame that betrayed her,   5075
For she has no one else to help.
This lady, deprived of her entire
Inheritance by her sister, hopes
To win her suit through you.
You're the only one she wants.   5080
Nothing could ever persuade her
That anyone else could help.
You'll win the love of this friendless,
Cheated woman, and vastly
Increase your renown, if you win her   5085
Back what is rightfully hers!
She herself would have sought you,
Hoping for this kindness, and no one
Could have taken her place, except
That illness has kept her away,   5090
Forced her to take to her bed.
Now tell me, please, if you dare
To come as she asks, or if
You'll choose to say no and do nothing."
"No," he answered, "saying   5095
No wins no man fame.
No more will I say no,
But follow you, sweet friend!
Gladly, wherever you please.

And if she for whom you've sought me   5100
Truly needs me, have
No fear. Anything I'm able
To do for her, I'll do.
May God give me the grace
And the great good luck to win her   5105
Back what is rightly hers!"

So riding along, side
By side, and chatting, they approached
The Castle of Infinite Misfortune.
They had no interest in passing   5110
It by, for the sun was setting.
So they rode up to the castle,
And the people who saw them come
Shouted and yelled at the knight:
"Curses on your coming, curses!   5115
Whoever showed you this lodging
Meant to harm you, and shame you.
An abbot could swear it's the truth."
"You foolish, vulgar people,"
He answered, "filled with evil   5120
And utterly empty of good,
Why attack me like this?"
"Why? Oh, you'll find out,
If you go a little bit farther.
But you can't find out here: 5125
You'll have to go in there,
You'll have to enter that castle."
And at once he started toward the tower,
And all the people shouted,
All of them, at the top of their lungs: 5130
"Don't look for trouble! Where are you

Going? If you've ever known anyone
Who's harmed you, and shamed you, that's
What they'll do, there where you're headed,
And you'll never live to tell it."   5135
"You shameless, wicked people,"
Answered Yvain, hearing them,
"Insolent, wretched: have you any
Reason for attacking me? What
Are you asking for, what is it you want?   5140
Why are you muttering at my heels?"
"My friend! There's no reason for anger,"
Said a lady well on in years,
Plainly sensible and polite.
"Surely, there's no harm in their words.   5145
They're only trying to warn you,
If only you'd try to understand,
That you ought not seek shelter there.
But they dare not tell you why.
They're simply warning and scolding,   5150
Trying to make you afraid.
They do this for every stranger,
All the time, to keep them
From ever entering the castle.
And it's also our custom never   5155
To dare give lodging or shelter
To any noble gentleman,
To no one who comes here from anywhere
Else. It's up to you.
No one will stop you from going.   5160
Go up, if you choose to—but my
Advice is: turn back." "Lady!"
He said. "I suspect there is honor
And sense in your words, if only
I were able to do as you say.   5165
But I've no idea where else

I might find lodging for tonight."
"Dear me!" she said. "I'll be still.
It's really none of my business.
Go wherever you please!   5170
Still, I'd be more than happy
To see you come back from in there
Not too much disgraced. But that
Is simply too much to expect."
"Lady!" he answered. "May God   5175
Be your saviour! But my foolish heart
Leads me on, and I obey my heart."
And he went straight up to the gate,
He and his lion and the girl.
And then the porter called out,   5180
Saying: "Quick! Quick!
You're coming to a place that will well
And truly lock you up:
And may your coming be cursed!"

And after greeting him this way   5185
The porter hurried on up,
But the greeting was deeply insulting.
Yet my lord Yvain said nothing,
And went right on, and found
A great high hall, brand new,   5190
With a walled courtyard in front of it,
And a wall of great sharpened stakes,
And inside, behind the stakes,
He saw three hundred girls
All sewing away, some working   5195
With golden thread, some silk,
Working as hard as they could.
But their wretched poverty was such

That they sat there bareheaded, many
So poor that they wore no sash,   5200
And their dresses were torn at the breast
And out at the elbows, and their shifts
Were dirty around the neck.
And their necks were thin, and their faces
Pale with hunger and misery.   5205
He saw them, and they saw him,
And they bowed their heads, and they wept,
And for a long, long time did not move,
Knowing there was nothing to be done,
Unable to raise their eyes   5210
From the ground, so bent with sorrow.
And after watching them a while
My lord Yvain turned
And headed back toward the gate,
And the porter jumped in front of him   5215
And cried: "You're wasting your time:
There's no way out, good sir!
You'd rather be out than in,
But by my head it's no use!
First you'll have your fill   5220
Of disgrace—more than you'll think
You can bear. It wasn't terribly
Intelligent, coming in here,
For now there's no way out."
"Good brother, I've no wish to leave!   5225
But tell me, by your father's soul:
These ladies I see in the courtyard,
Weaving cloth of silk
And brocade, where are they from?
Their work is excellent, it pleases me,   5230
But it makes me distinctly unhappy
To see how their faces and their bodies
Are so thin and pale and wretched.

It seems to me they'd be graceful
And lovely, if they had the sort   5235
Of things they'd like to have."
"And I will tell you nothing,"
He said. "Find someone else!"
"I shall, since I've nothing better."
And then he looked for the door   5240
Of that courtyard where the girls were working,
And went in among them, and greeted
Them all, and saw tears
Falling from their eyes, streaming
Down from their eyes, all of them   5245
Sitting and weeping together.
And he said: "May it please our Lord
That this sorrow, whatever it comes from,
Be taken from your hearts and turned
Into joy!" And one of them answered: 5250
"May the God you've prayed to hear you!
Nor will we conceal who
We are and where we're from.
I assume that is your request?"
"That," he said, "is why   5255
I came here." "My lord! Long ago
The King of the Island of Virgins
Went hunting gossip and stories
In many courts and in many
Countries, travelling like a fool   5260
Till he stumbled across this dangerous
Place. What an unlucky hour!
For the shame and misery we've known,
We miserable prisoners that you see,
Was nothing we'd ever deserved.   5265
And believe me, you can expect
Exactly the same for yourself,
If they won't let you be ransomed!

But be all that as it may,
Our king came to this castle,   5270
Owned by two sons of the devil—
And that's not nonsense, believe me!
They'd been born of a woman and a demon.
And these two were ready to fight
With the king, who was frightened silly,   5275
For he was barely eighteen
And they could have cut him in half
Like a soft and juicy lamb.
So the king, consumed with terror,
Escaped as best he was able,   5280
Swearing that every year
He'd send them thirty young girls,
While the agreement lasted. And paying
This tribute set him free.
And the terms he swore to provided   5285
That this tribute should last as long
As this pair of demons lived,
Except that on the day
They were beaten in battle the tribute
Should end for ever, and all   5290
Of us would be freed, who now
Are bound to live in shame
And sadness and misery. None of us
Will ever know pleasure again.
For I spoke like a child and a fool,   5295
Speaking as I did of freedom.
None of us will ever leave.
We'll spend our days weaving
Silk, and wearing rags.
We'll spend our days poor   5300
And naked and hungry and thirsty,
For they'll never pay us what we earn,
Let us buy better food.

We've only a bit of bread,
Some in the morning and less   5305
At night. Our work doesn't pay
Any of us even as much
As four pennies in a single day.
And that's not enough to feed us
Or put clothes on our backs. Even   5310
Earning twenty sous
A week, we're still miserable,
We never escape it. It's true:
There isn't one of us here
Who doesn't earn twenty or more—   5315
And that's as rich as a duke!
And yet we're miserably poor,
And the ones we work for are rich
Because of what we produce.
We work most nights, and we work   5320
All day, just to stay alive,
For they threaten to cut off our arms
And legs if we rest. No one
Dares to rest. But why
Go on telling you these things?   5325
We've so much misery and shame
I couldn't tell you a fifth of it.
And what makes us wild with grief
Is seeing the death of so many
Rich and worthy knights,   5330
Who come to fight these demons.
Their lodging is exceedingly costly,
As yours will be, tomorrow,
For whether you like it or not
You'll have to fight them, alone   5335
And singlehanded, fight
And then lose your fame to those demons."
"May God, who is heavenly truth,

Protect," said my lord Yvain,
"And give you back honor and joy,   5340
If so He wishes it to be!
But now I'm obliged to go see
The people who live in this castle,
And find out how they'll receive me."
"Go then, my lord! May He keep you,   5345
Who bestows all goodness and blessings!"

And then he went to the hall
And found no one, good or evil,
Who could say a word. So they went
All through the house, till they found   5350
Themselves in a garden. No one
Had ever spoken of stabling
Their horses: not a word had been said.
Did it matter? They were very well stabled
By those who thought they now owned them.   5355
It's not my place to judge:
The horses' owners were still healthy
And well. But the horses had oats
And hay and straw right up
To their bellies. And Yvain went into   5360
The garden, and the girl and the lion
Went after him. And he saw a gentleman,
Propped up on his elbow, lying
On a silken cloth, and a girl
Was reading him from some romance,   5365
I have no idea about whom.
And in order to hear this romance
A lady had come to lie there
With them. She was the girl's

Mother, and the gentleman her father.   5370
And both of them were right to rejoice
At seeing her and hearing her read,
For she was their only child,
Not yet quite seventeen
And so beautiful, graceful, and lovely   5375
That the God of Love would have bound
Himself to her service, if he'd seen her,
And never let her fall
In love with anyone but him.
And he would have become a man,   5380
And set aside his godhood,
And struck his own body with that dart
Whose wound never heals
(Unless some unfaithful doctor
Cures it). But no one should ever   5385
Be cured, except by unfaithfulness.
And anyone cured by anything
Different was never truly
In love. I could tell you so much
Of this wound, if you wanted to listen,   5390
That I couldn't finish my story
Today. But there'd surely be someone
Saying I was talking nonsense,
For people are no longer lovers,
And can't love as they used to love,   5395
And don't want to hear it talked of.
So listen, now, and hear
How Yvain was welcomed, what greeting
He got, and how it was given.
Everyone there in that garden   5400
Leaped to their feet when they saw him.
As soon as they saw him they cried
With one voice: "This way, good sir!
Whatever blessings God

Can pronounce or bestow, may they come   5405
To you and anyone you love!"
I haven't the faintest idea
If they lied, but they welcomed him happily
And seemed to be pleased that he
Could be lodged with them, and lodged well.   5410
Even the lord's daughter
Served him with honor, behaving
As one should to a worthy guest.
She helped him off with his armor,
Nor was that the least she did,   5415
For she washed his face and his neck
With her very own hands. And the lord
Of the house insisted that every
Honor be shown him, and so
It was. She took a pleated   5420
Shirt from her storage chest,
And white stockings, and a needle
And thread to sew on the sleeves,
And did so. He was dressed: God keep
This service from becoming too costly!   5425
And she gave him a good coat
To wear over his shirt,
And a red furred cloak, fashionably
Cut, to wrap round his neck,
And was so attentive in every   5430
Way that he grew embarrassed.
But the girl was so open and courteous,
So plainly kind and good,
That she thought she had done very little.
And further, she knew perfectly   5435
Well that her mother wished nothing
Undone that might possibly please him.
That night they brought him so much
To eat that he could not eat everything.

The men at arms who carried   5440
The dishes must have been angry.
And at bedtime they served him with such
High honor that he lay down in comfort,
And no one dared to come near him
Once he had taken to his bed.   5445
The lion lay at his feet,
As he always did. And in
The morning, when God lit up
His light, for the world to see with,
Yvain got out of bed   5450
As quickly and quietly and early
As he could, without disturbing
The household, and he and the girl
Went to the chapel and heard
Mass, which the priest said   5455
At once, to the Holy Ghost's honor.

And after the Mass my lord
Yvain was given bad news,
Thinking the time had come
To leave, and nothing would stop him.   5460
But it did not go as he wished.
He said to his host: "Lord,
I shall leave you, with your permission."
And the lord of the house answered:
"My friend! I cannot grant it,   5465
Not yet. And I have a reason.
An exceedingly cruel and devilish
Rule prevails in this castle,
And I am obliged to uphold it.
I shall call two of my soldiers,   5470
Great strapping fellows, and strong,

And right or wrong, you
Are obliged to fight them both.
If you can fight them off,
If you can defeat and kill them,   5475
My daughter wants you as a husband,
And this castle, and all the lands
And honors that go with it, will be yours."
"Lord!" said Yvain. "It's not
What I wish. God will not give her   5480
To me, she will stay with you,
For she is beautiful enough,
And good, and well bred, that the Emperor
Of Germany would do well to win her!"
"Be still, my dear guest!" said his host.   5485
"There's no point to listening to you speak,
For there's nothing you can do to escape.
Whoever can defeat these two,
Who are shortly going to attack you,
Will have my castle, and my daughter   5490
As his wife, and all my lands.
The battle will take place;
Nothing in the world can prevent it.
But I do understand why
You refuse my daughter. It's cowardice.   5495
You think it will let you out
Of the battle. Nonsense. Believe me,
Sir, nothing will get you
Out of it, for this battle must be!
No knight who takes lodging here   5500
Can ever escape it. This
Is our custom, and a settled rule
I expect will last a long time,
For my daughter will never be married
Until they're conquered, or dead."   5505
"In which case I'm obliged to fight them,

In spite of myself. And yet,
I assure you, I'd gladly forgo
This battle. I regret it. But let
It be, since it can't be helped."   5510
And then two black, hideous
Sons of the devil came in,
And all their weapons were a pair
Of jagged dogwood clubs,
Made ready for war with a covering   5515
Of copper and wound around
With brass. Their armor extended
From the shoulders all the way
To their knees, but their heads
And faces were bare. And their legs,   5520
Not particularly slender
Or weak, were also bare.
And ready for war they came at him,
Holding in front of their faces
Light, strong shields.   5525
And then the lion began
To quiver, seeing them. He knew
Perfectly well that the weapons
They were carrying were meant to be used
Against his lord and master.   5530
His hair stood up, his mane
Bristled, and he shook with anger
And beat the ground with his tail,
Ready and eager to save
His master, before they could kill him.   5535
And seeing the lion, they said:
"Knight! That lion is threatening
Us. Get him away.
Surrender, here and now,
Or else you've got to put him   5540
Someplace where he can't join

In this fight, either by helping
You or injuring us.
We play this game by ourselves!
That lion would be very glad   5545
To help you, if we let him."
"Take him away yourselves,
If he frightens you!" declared Yvain.
"It would suit me perfectly well
If he hurt you as much as he could.   5550
I'd much appreciate his help."
"By God!" they exclaimed. "It won't do.
You're not having help from him.
You've got to do your best
Alone, without assistance!   5555
It's only you against us.
If that lion fights at your side,
If that lion attacks us, it won't
Be simply you against us,
But two against two. Do   5560
As we tell you. Your lion has got
To be put away, and now,
And whether you like it or not."
"And where," said he, "should I put him?
Where would you like him to be?"   5565
So they showed him a tiny room,
And said: "Lock him in there!"
"Exactly as you wish," said Yvain.
And he led him in and locked
The door. And they brought Yvain   5570
His weapons and body armor,
And led out his horse and handed him
The reins, and Yvain mounted.
Sure of their safety from the lion,
Locked away in that room,   5575
The two devilish champions

Came forward, determined to harm him
And shame him. They hit him hard
With their clubs, and his shield and helmet
Weren't much help. When they smashed   5580
Away at his helmet, it was quickly
Dented, and began to crack,
And his shield splintered like a mirror:
They battered such holes that a fist
Could have shoved right through them.   5585
They were truly after him, those two.
And what did Yvain do
To those devils? Fear and shame
Drove him to fight with all
His strength. Fired up and struggling,   5590
He dealt them crashing blows,
Returning presents as good
As he'd gotten, doubling their kindness.
And the lion, locked in his room,
Was troubled and sad at heart,   5595
Remembering Yvain's goodness,
And his generous help, and knowing
How badly the knight needed
His lion's help, and now.
He could pay him back in full measure,   5600
Even double and redouble his kindness,
Leaving no debt unpaid,
If only he could get himself out.
He searched in every corner
And found nothing, no way   5605
Of escaping. And hearing how fierce
And desperate and dangerous the battle
Had become, his sorrow drove him
Mad with despair. Hunting
Again and again, he found   5610
That near the ground the threshold

Was rotting, and he clawed at it, and squeezed
Partly through. But his back
Wedged in, and stuck. And Yvain
Was weary and sweating hard,   5615
Finding the two assassins
Tough and strong and dangerous.
He'd taken many blows,
And returned as many as he could,
And they still came at him, unharmed.   5620
They were skilled, experienced fighters,
And their shields weren't the sort
That any sword could cut through,
No matter how hard or how sharp.
Yvain was very well   5625
Aware that they might kill him,
But he managed to hold his own
Until the lion got out,
Clawing under the threshold.
And now those fiends could be beaten—   5630
Or never at all. There'd be
No truce between them and the lion
For as long as he saw them still living.
He leaped on one and dragged him
To the ground like a sack of wheat.   5635
Both the demons were terrified,
But no one else in that place
Could keep from rejoicing. When the lion
Had him down, nothing
Could put him back on his feet   5640
Unless the other one helped him.
And he ran to assist him, carefully
Guarding himself, worried
That the lion would turn on him
As soon as he'd killed the one   5645
He'd thrown to the ground. He was far more

Afraid of the lion than the lion's
Master. But Yvain would
Have been out of his mind, once the fellow
Turned his back, and his neck   5650
Was nicely exposed and available,
If he'd let him live much longer.
Things were working out well.
Seeing that bare head
And naked neck, he gave him   5655
Such a stroke with his sword
That the head was so smoothly sliced
Off the shoulders that its owner never
Knew it. And now he dismounted,
Wanting to rescue the other one   5660
From the lion's jaws. In vain:
He'd been injured so badly that no doctor
Could ever help him. The lion
Had charged so furiously, so wildly,
That his wounds were terrible. As soon   5665
As Yvain had pushed the lion
Off, he could see that the shoulder
Had been ripped completely away
From the body. But nothing he saw
Made Yvain feel sorry. The club   5670
Had fallen from his hand, and he lay
On the ground, almost a corpse,
Unable to move or fight.
But still, he was able to speak,
And he said, as well as he could: 5675
"Take away your lion, good sir!
Don't let him hurt me any more.
For now you can do with me
Exactly as you please, and anyone
Who begs for mercy must always   5680
Be granted it whenever it's asked for,

Unless the victor is a man
Without pity. I can't defend myself—
Indeed, I can't even rise
And leave this place, unaided.   5685
I surrender myself to your mercy."
"You admit defeat," asked Yvain,
"Concede that you're conquered and beaten?"
"Lord: that seems to be obvious.
In spite of myself, I've been beaten.   5690
I freely concede defeat."
"Then you've nothing to fear from me,
And my lion, too, grants you
Your safety." Then they rushed to Yvain,
Everyone crowding around him,   5695
And the lord and his lady both
Embraced him, and rejoiced, and spoke
Of their daughter, telling him:
"And now you shall be lord
And master of us all, and our daughter   5700
Will be your lady. We give you
Our daughter as your wife." "And I,"
He replied, "give her back.
Who has her, should keep her! It's none
Of my business. I speak without scorn.   5705
Don't be distressed because
I refuse her. I cannot take her,
I must not. But give me, please,
The girls you're holding captive!
The agreement so stipulates, and it's time,   5710
As you know, that they must be freed."
"You're right," he said, "that's true,
And I hand them over. They're yours.
There's nothing to argue about.
But you'd also do well to take   5715
My daughter, and all my wealth,

For she's beautiful, and noble, and wise!
You're hardly likely to find
Another marriage as rich
As this one." "Lord! My legal   5720
Obligations, and all my affairs,
Are unknown to you. I dare not explain.
But understand this: what I
Refuse would never be declined
By anyone who could follow his heart   5725
And accept so lovely and noble
A girl, receive her freely,
As I would do, were I free
To take this one or any other.
But I can't. Believe me, I can't.   5730
Allow me to leave you in peace!
For the lady awaits me, she
Who came here with me. She
And I have travelled long
And far, and I wish to stand by her,   5735
Whatever the future may bring me."
"Leave, good sir? But how?
Never, unless I command it,
And it's my decision not to.
For you, my gates are not open.   5740
No. You'll stay here, my prisoner.
You're arrogant, sir, and unjust,
When I beg you to take my daughter
And you scorn her, disdain her." "Scorn her,
Lord? Not so, by my soul!   5745
Whatever it costs me, I cannot
Remain, and I cannot marry.
I must follow the lady who leads me:
Everything else is impossible.
But believe me, I can pledge you with this   5750
My right hand, as sure as you see me

Now, that I shall return,
If ever I can, and be glad
To accept your daughter, if
And when you think it right."   5755
"Anyone be damned who asks you
For your pledge, or your faith, or your promise!
If my daughter pleased you, you'd be back here
Quickly enough. No oath
And no pledge would bring you back   5760
Any sooner, by God. Go, then!
I release you from all your promises
And all your agreements. Whatever
May keep you away, wind
Or rain or nothing at all,   5765
I don't care. Could I think so poorly
Of my daughter that I'd force you to have her?
Now go and do what you need to!
It's all the same to me
Whether you go or you stay."   5770

And Yvain turned quickly away
And stayed no longer in that castle.
And he led away with him
Those miserable wretches, now free,
Poor, and dressed in rags,   5775
That the lord had given to his custody.
How rich they felt themselves,
All of them leaving that castle,
Filing out in pairs.
And I think they'd have felt no greater   5780
Joy if He who made them,
He who made the whole world,
Had descended from heaven to earth.

And all the people who'd insulted him
And shamed him, as much as they'd been able,   5785
Now begged his forgiveness, and for peace,
And sought to escort him on his way.
And he answered that their words meant nothing.
"I don't understand what you're saying,"
He said. "There's nothing to be settled,   5790
As between us. I can't recall
Any unpleasant words."
This pleased them immensely, and all of them
Loudly praised his courtesy,
And having taken him a long way   5795
Along on his road, commended him
To God. And the girls he'd freed
Asked his permission to leave.
As they said their farewell they bowed
And prayed for him, hoping God   5800
Would grant him joy and health
And whatever his heart wished for,
Wherever he might choose to go.
Not wanting to linger, he replied
That he hoped God would save   5805
Them all. "Go!" he said.
"May God bring you home happy
And safe!" So off they went
On their way, journeying joyfully
—And Yvain immediately hurried   5810
In the opposite direction, riding
As fast as he could, never
Stopping, going as the girl
Directed, seven days in the week.
She knew the road exceedingly   5815
Well, and knew the refuge
Where she'd left the afflicted, disconsolate
Woman who'd lost her inheritance.

And yet when she heard the news
That the girl was back, and with her   5820
The Knight of the Lion, there'd never
Been such joy as her heart
Felt, convinced that now,
If she pressed her case, her older
Sister would surely concede her   5825
Some share of their father's estate.
She'd been ill a very long time,
And was just risen from her sickbed,
But the illness had been long and hard
And had seriously harmed her, as anyone   5830
Could see, looking at her face.
At their first meeting she went
Directly out to welcome them,
Greeting them and showing them honor
In every way she could.   5835
There's no need to speak
Of the joy in the house, that night.
To do more than mention it would prolong
My story to no purpose. Permit me
To pass over it and go to the following   5840
Day, when they mounted their horses
And left. And they rode till they saw
The castle where King Arthur had been staying
For several weeks or more.
And the lady who'd disinherited   5845
Her sister was there, staying
Near the court, awaiting
Her sister's arrival, which was closer
Than she could have known. But it made
No difference to her, for she thought   5850
The younger woman would never
Find anyone able
To stand up to Gawain in battle,

And only a single day
Of the forty were left to her. The inheritance   5855
Would have been hers alone,
Legally absolute,
In justice and according to the king's
Judgment, had that day gone by.
But more stood in her way   5860
Than she could have known or believed.

They slept that night outside
The castle town, in a small,
Poor house, where no one knew them,
For had they stayed at the castle   5865
Everyone would have known them,
And they were careful to keep that from happening.
As soon as dawn broke they had
To leave, of course, but they hid
Themselves, concealing their presence   5870
Till the sun was high and bright.

I can't tell you how many
Days had gone by since Gawain
Vanished, and no one at court
Had any idea where he was,   5875
Except the lady he was bound
To fight for. He'd slipped away,
Three or even four leagues
From court, and when he returned
He'd equipped himself so that no one   5880
Could ever have known him, though they'd seen
And heard him every day:

His weapons and armor were so different.
And the lady, whose wrongful conduct
Toward her sister was clearly apparent,   5885
Brought him to court in the sight
Of all, intending to use him
To prevail in a dispute where she had
No right. "Your Majesty!" she said.
"Time passes. Noon will soon   5890
Be gone, and today's the last day.
You see how I'm ready to assert
My rights. If my sister meant
To return, we'd have no choice
But to await her coming. But I'm thankful   5895
To God on high that she's never
Coming back. Plainly,
She can't do better than she's done,
And all her effort's been wasted.
As for me, I've always been ready—   5900
Down to this very last moment—
To defend what's rightly mine.
I've won my claim without fighting,
And now it's mine, and I'll go
And enjoy my inheritance in peace.   5905
I've no need at all to answer
To my sister, not for the rest
Of my life. She can live miserably,
And in sorrow." And the king, knowing
Quite well that the lady was grossly   5910
Unfair and disloyal to her sister,
Answered: "My friend! In a royal
Court one waits, by God,
As long as the king's justice
Thinks proper for reaching a verdict.   5915
There'll be nothing fast and loose:
It seems to me there's still

Plenty of time for your sister
To come." And as he spoke
The king saw the Knight   5920
Of the Lion, and the girl with him.
They'd come ahead, those two,
Stealing away from the lion,
Who'd remained at their lodging.

And seeing the younger sister,   5925
Whom of course he knew, he was very
Pleased, and even delighted,
That she'd come in time, for he held
Her side of the quarrel, because
He respected justice and right.   5930
And he spoke of his pleasure, as soon
As he found himself able: "Come forward,
Pretty one! May God save you!"
When the other heard him, she started,
And turned, and saw the knight   5935
Her sister had brought with her
To fight for her rights, and her face
Became blacker than the blackest earth.
But everyone welcomed the younger
Sister, who went to the king   5940
And stood before his chair,
And standing in front of him, said:
"God save the king and his court!
Your majesty! If any knight
Can defend my rights and establish   5945
My claims, this knight will accomplish it.
He has followed me here only
Out of pity for my plight. He has much
To occupy him, elsewhere, this gracious,

Generous courtier of high birth.   5950
But he felt so sorry for me
That he's put aside his other
Concerns in favor of mine.
My dear sister, whom I love
As I love myself, would do   5955
The right and courteous thing
If she let me have what was mine,
Only what was mine, and made peace
Between us. I want nothing that's hers."
"And I," said the other, "want nothing   5960
That's yours, for that's what you have
And will have. No preaching will do it,
For preaching will get you nothing.
May your sadness dry you to dust."
And the other, who knew how   5965
To be pleasant, and was wise as well
As courteous, answered at once:
"Surely," she said, "it saddens me
That two knights the like of these
Should fight because of us,   5970
And because of so slight a quarrel.
But I can't give up my rights;
My need is far too great.
It would show far more goodwill
If you simply gave me what I deserve."   5975
"Hah!" said the other. "Anyone
Who listened to you would be stupid.
May I burn in the fires of hell
If I give you anything for your comfort!
The banks of the Seine will come   5980
Together, and morning will be noon,
If I don't make you do battle."
"May God, in whom I trust
And have trusted all the days of my life,

And trust now, and the right, which is mine,   5985
Give their help to him
Who for charity and noble generosity
Has put himself at my service,
Though he does not know me and I
Know neither his name nor him."   5990

So they talked till their words had ended,
And then they led their knights
To the middle of the court. And everyone
Came running to see them, as people
Usually come running when they want   5995
To see a fight up close,
And watch the blows. But those
Who were soon to fight could not
Recognize each other, though they'd always
Loved one another dearly.   6000
Did they love one another now?
I could answer you "Yes" or "No,"
And either one would be right,
As I shall proceed to prove.
Truly, Gawain loved   6005
Yvain, and thought him his friend,
As Yvain thought him, had he known
Who he was. Even here, had he known him,
He'd have shown him honor and respect.
He'd have laid down his life for him,   6010
As Gawain would have done for Yvain,
Rather than harm his friend.
Could love be more perfect or finer?
Not a bit. But their hate, on the other
Hand, was just as obvious.   6015
Indeed: it's perfectly clear

That one would have broken the other's
Head, and cheerfully, and tried
To do his best to do
The worst he could to disgrace him.   6020
Incredible! What an absolute marvel,
Love and mortal Hate
Found in a single basket.
God! How can two things
So utterly unlike find   6025
Themselves at home together?
Impossible, it seems to me:
They could not share the same roof,
And if they tried living
Together, there'd surely be quarreling   6030
And commotion, as soon as each
Knew the other was there.
And yet the house could have many
Rooms, bedrooms, and galleries,
And it might well be like that: 6035
I suppose Love could hide
In some out-of-the-way room, and Hate
Go up on balconies hung
Over highways and streets, choosing
To exhibit herself in public.   6040
Hate has her bow ready
To shoot, and she sits in the saddle
And gallops at Love as hard
As she can, and Love doesn't move.
Love! Where are you hiding?   6045
Come out! See what an ally
Your friends' enemies have led
To the field, to battle against you.
These very same men are those enemies,
Loving each other with a saintly   6050
Love, for Love's never false,

But a precious thing, and holy.
But Love's gone totally blind,
And Hate's no better off.
If Love had had any idea   6055
Just who they were, he would have
Forbidden them to harm each other,
To do anything dangerous or hurtful.
So love is blind, but more
Than blind, disconsolate and deluded: 6060
Even seeing them straight on
He can't tell which ones are his.
And Hate hasn't a notion
Why either should hate the other,
But he wants to set them at odds,   6065
Make each one hate with a mortal
Hate. And, of course, no one
Can love a man he longs
To disgrace and wants to kill.
What then? Is Yvain determined   6070
To kill Gawain, his friend?
Yes, and Gawain the same.
Would Gawain want to kill
Yvain with his very own hands,
Or perhaps do worse things still?   6075
Not really: I swear it, on oath.
Neither would really want
To injure or shame the other,
Not for everything God has done
For man, not for all the wealth   6080
Of Rome. But of course I'm lying.
Clearly, as anyone could see,
They were ready to attack each other,
Lances high and ready,
Prepared to slash at each other,   6085
To do all the damage they could,

And nothing held back. Now tell me:
Whoever gets the worst of it,
Whichever one is beaten
In battle, who can he blame?   6090
It worries me, for I'm quite convinced
If they come to blows they'll never
Stop their struggling and fighting
Till someone has won a victory.
Would Yvain be able to say,   6095
If he were the one who lost,
That he'd been hurt and disgraced
By someone who calls him his friend,
Someone who never mentions
His name except in friendship?   6100
And suppose it went the other
Way, and Yvain did the harm,
Would Gawain, who'd then be defeated,
Be able to complain of his friend?
Hardly: he wouldn't know who did it.   6105
But neither knew the other,
And so they drew back, and made ready.
Their lances shattered, when they met,
Good lances, made out of ashwood.
Not a word was spoken, for had   6110
They exchanged as much as a single
Word, they'd have met quite differently.
Then, there'd have been no blows
From spears or swords, but arms
Would be wound in embraces, and kisses   6115
Given, instead of wounds.
And now they went at it for real.
Their swords were hardly improved,
Nor their helmets, nor their shields, all badly
Dented, and split, and their sharpened   6120
Blades chipped and notched,

And considerably blunted, for they struck
At each other, not with the flat
Of their weapons, but the deadly blades,
And they hacked so hard at the other's   6125
Neck, and nose-guard, and forehead,
And cheeks, that both were purple
And discolored, there under
The skin where the blood had clotted.
And their long coats of mail were torn,   6130
And their shields so broken up
That both of them were wounded.
And they fought so hard, and so fiercely,
That both were panting and short
Of breath, as the battle went on.   6135
Every jewel set
In their helmets was crushed to powder,
Smashed to bits, as the blows
Crashed on their heads, both of them   6140
Stunned, their brains nearly beaten
Out. Their eyes sparkled
As with massive, heavy fists
And powerful muscles, and strong
Bones, they swung at each other   6145
As long as their hands could hold
Their swords, useful tools
For the sort of damage they were doing.

Weary, after a long time,
Their helmets battered in,   6150
Their linked mail-coats coming
Apart from the fierce sword strokes,
Their shields split and half shattered,
They drew back a bit,

Letting their blood cool   6155
And trying to recover their breath.
But not for very long.
And then they fell on each other
Even more furiously than before.
And everyone said that two   6160
More courageous knights had never
Existed. "This is no game.
These two are fighting in earnest.
But how could they ever be paid
What they're worth, and what they deserve?"   6165
And the two friends who were fighting
Heard these words, and heard
How courtiers were trying to make peace
Between the two sisters, but in vain,
For the older sister wanted   6170
No part of any peace.
The younger one said she'd leave it
To the king, and accept his judgment,
Not quibbling whatever he decided,
But the older was so malicious   6175
That even Queen Guinevere
And all the knights and the king
And the ladies and all the townsfolk
Began to favor the younger,
And went to the king, and begged him   6180
To give her at least a third
Or a fourth of their father's estate,
In spite of the older one's claim,
And asked him to part the two knights,
Who had shown such wonderful courage.   6185
What a shame it would be, they declared,
If either were seriously hurt
Or deprived of any honor.
But the king said that peace

Was not for him to establish;   6190
The older sister spurned it,
For her spirit was mean. And everything
They said was heard by both
Knights, who had gone on fighting
So savagely that everyone marvelled,   6195
For the battle had gone so evenly
That no one could possibly have said
Who was winner or loser.
And even the two who were fighting,
Earning honor with martyrdom,   6200
Were astonished and unable to grasp it,
For they fought on such equal terms
That each one found it miraculous
For anyone to stand against him
So fiercely and long and well.   6205
They fought so exceedingly long
That day began to turn night,
And each of them fought with weary
Arms and wretched body,
And their overheated blood   6210
Boiled out of many wounds
And ran down their mail-coats.
No wonder they both wanted
To rest: they had fought magnificently.
So each of them rested a bit,   6215
Thinking to himself that at last
He'd met his match, no matter
How long he'd waited to find it.
They rested longer than they meant to,
Not daring to begin again.   6220
Fighting no longer interested them,
As much for the growing darkness
As for the fear they felt for each other.
Both things kept them apart

And urged them to preserve their new peace.   6225
But before they left that field
They'd find out just who they were,
And both would be happy, and sorry.

Yvain was the first to speak,
Brave and courteous as he was.   6230
But even his friend couldn't tell
It was him, for his voice was weak,
And his words could barely be heard,
Hoarse, and feeble, and low.
All the blows he'd received   6235
Had badly shaken him. "Lord!"
He began. "Night approaches.
No one, I think, will blame
Or reproach us if darkness keeps us
Apart. And I will admit   6240
That I fear and value you immensely.
Never in all my life
Have I fought so painful a battle,
Nor have I ever seen
A knight I so much wanted   6245
To know. You know how to strike
Your blows, and you use them well.
No knight I've ever known
Can fight so punishingly. I had no
Desire to spend this day   6250
Experiencing the blows you've given me.
You've half addled my head."
"Good lord!" Gawain answered.
"You're no more exhausted and stunned
Than I am, and perhaps even less.   6255
And if I knew you, knight,

I hope you'd not be displeased.
And indeed, if I've given you anything
You've paid me back in full,
Principal and interest too.   6260
You were readier to pay me in kind
Than I was anxious to receive it.
But let that be as it will.
And since you've asked me to tell you
The name I go by, I'll not   6265
Keep it hidden. My name
Is Gawain, son of King Lot."
As soon as Yvain heard him
He was bewildered and deeply disturbed.
Wild with rage, he threw   6270
His blood-covered sword to the ground,
And then his cracked and shattered
Shield after it, and dismounted
From his horse, and approaching on foot
He cried: "Dear God! What bad luck!   6275
What kind of stupid mistake
Brought on this battle, neither
Of us knowing the other.
Had I known who you were, nothing
Could have made me fight with you.   6280
Believe me, I'd have surrendered to you
And never struck a blow."
"What?" Gawain exclaimed.
"Who are you?" "I am Yvain,
Who loves you better than anyone   6285
In the world, however far
It may stretch, for everywhere we've been
You've always loved me, and honored me.
And I wish to do you such honor,
And make you such amends, in this business,   6290
That I declare myself defeated."

"You'd do so much for me?"
Said my sweet lord Gawain.
"How insolent I'd be, how presumptuous,
To accept what you'd give me so freely.   6295
No such honor shall be mine.
It belongs to you, it's yours."
"Never, good sir! Never!
How could I possibly accept it?
I can't continue. I'm utterly   6300
Defeated, my wounds are too serious."
"Never let that worry you!"
Cried his friend and companion.
"It's I who've been conquered and beaten.
And there's no flattery in my words.   6305
There's no stranger, anywhere in the world,
To whom I'd not say as much,
Rather than endure more fighting."
And as he spoke he dismounted,
And each embraced the other,   6310
And kissed the other, their arms
Around each other's necks,
Each continuing to insist
That he'd lost. They were arguing away
When the king and all the barons   6315
Came running from all around them,
Seeing them reconciled,
All of them anxious to hear
How it had happened, and who
Were these happily embracing knights.   6320
"Gentlemen!" said the king. "Tell us,
Please, how you've come to such friendship
And understanding, after
A day filled with such hatred
And incredible combat!" And Gawain,   6325
His nephew, answered the king:

"Your majesty! Nothing will be kept from you,
Neither the exceeding bad luck
Nor the misfortune that brought us
This battle. And since you've bothered   6330
To approach us, seeking to know
The truth, you shall surely hear it.
I, Gawain, your nephew,
Did not know my friend and companion,
My lord Yvain, who this is,   6335
Until, by the gracious mercy
Of God, he asked me my name.
And we told each other our names,
And knew each other at last,
But only after we'd fought.   6340
We fought well. Had
Our combat gone on just
A little longer, surely
It would have gone badly for me,
For by my head he'd have killed me,   6345
Both because of his skill
And because of the wrong I was chosen
To fight for. I'd rather my friends
Beat me in battle than killed me."
Then Yvain's blood was up,   6350
And he answered at once: "My dear
Friend! So help me God,
Everything you've said is wrong.
The king, our lord, should know
That without a doubt I   6355
Am the one who was beaten in this combat!"
"No, I." "No, I," they kept saying,
Both so noble and generous
That they passed the victory and the crown
Back and forth, neither of them   6360
Willing to accept it, each of them

Trying as hard as he could
To convince the king and the court
That he was the one who'd been beaten.
But after listening a bit,   6365
The king ended their quarrel,
Wonderfully pleased by what
He had heard and seen that day,
And seeing them embracing each other,
Though before they'd hurt and wounded   6370
Each other all over their bodies.
"Gentlemen!" he declared. "You two
Love one another. And you show it,
Each one insisting he was beaten.
Now leave all this to me!   6375
I think I can arrange it all
So neatly that you'll both be honored,
And the world will praise my solution."
Both of them promised to do
Whatever he directed, exactly   6380
As he might order. And then
The king said he'd settle the quarrel
Fairly and also in good faith.
"Where," he asked, "is the lady
Who forcefully drove her sister   6385
From her lands, and disinherited her
By force and evil intent?"
"Lord!" she said. "I am here."
"You're there? Then come here! I saw
From the very beginning that you   6390
Were disinheriting her.
Her rights will not be denied:
You've just admitted the truth.
Now give her back what's hers:
You have no choice." "My lord!"   6395
She said. "If I spoke like a fool,

If I answered you like a simpleton,
You shouldn't take me literally.
Good God, your Majesty! Don't harm me!
You're a king, you ought to be careful   6400
About doing wrong and injustice."
"Exactly," said the king, "why I choose
To render justice to your sister.
It's not my custom to be unjust.
And surely you've heard how both   6405
Your knight and hers have left
Everything to my mercy. What
I shall say will not entirely
Please you, but everyone knows
You are wrong. Each knight claims   6410
Defeat, to honor the other one.
I've nothing to say about that.
Since everything's been left to me,
You will do exactly as I order
And in every single respect,   6415
Without objection, or I proclaim
My nephew beaten at arms.
Nothing could be worse for you,
And I'd contradict my own heart."
In fact, he'd never have said it,   6420
But he spoke in order to frighten her,
And to see if anything could frighten her
And oblige her, because of her fear,
To give back her sister's inheritance.
He was well and truly aware   6425
That nothing he could say would make her
Give back a thing, and only
Force or fear could oblige her.
And she was afraid, and cried out,
And said: "Good lord! I'm obliged   6430
To do precisely as you wish,

Though it grieves me, it breaks my heart.
But I'll do it, however it hurts,
And my sister will have what's hers.
And as pledge that she'll have her share   6435
Of our inheritance, I name you,
So she'll know it will truly be done."
"Then give it to her at once!"
Said the king, "and let her acknowledge
You as her lady, and honor you!   6440
Love her as you'd love anyone
Who serves you, and let her love you
As her lady and her older sister!"
And so the king arranged it,
And the girl took possession of her lands   6445
And offered him her gratitude. And then
The king spoke to his nephew,
That brave and valiant knight,
And asked that he let them disarm him,
And spoke to Yvain, and asked   6450
If he'd mind doing the same,
For now weapons and armor
Weren't needed. They laid down their arms,
And left the field as equals.
And then, taking off their armor,   6455
They saw the lion come running,
Searching everywhere for his master.
And as soon as he saw Yvain
He showed how happy he was.
The crowds melted away;   6460
Even the bravest left.
"All of you, stay!" cried Yvain.
"Why run? No one is chasing you.
Don't be afraid that that lion
Has any intention of hurting you!   6465
Please, believe me: he's mine,

As I am his. We two
Are companions, he and I."
Then all of them knew it was true,
As they'd heard it told, that this   6470
And no one else was the knight,
And also the lion, of whom
It was said that together they'd killed
The cruel giant. And my lord
Gawain said to Yvain: 6475
"My friend, so help me God,
You've thoroughly shamed me, today!
How terribly badly I've paid
You back for the service you rendered me,
Killing that giant and saving   6480
My nephews, and saving my niece.
I've thought a great deal about you,
Of late, and always with pain,
For everyone said we were friends
Who loved one another. I've thought   6485
Long, and I've thought hard,
And I never could understand,
For I'd never heard any talk
Of a knight I had known, anywhere
On earth, anywhere I'd been,   6490
Whose name was the Knight of the Lion.
I knew no one who used that name."
They removed their armor as they spoke,
And the lion came hurrying up
Toward his master, seated there,   6495
And as soon as he stood in front of him
Greeted him as a dumb beast can.
Then both knights had to be brought
To a sick room, for both of them needed
To have their wounds healed   6500
By a master surgeon and his plasters.

King Arthur, who loved them both,
Arranged it all. He sent for
A surgeon, who knew the science
Of healing wounds better   6505
Than anyone on earth. And the surgeon
Made it his business to care for them
Until, in the shortest time possible,
All of their wounds had been healed.

And then, when both were cured,   6510
My lord Yvain, whose heart
Was irrevocably set on love,
Saw clearly that he could not go on
But would have to die for love,
Unless his lady had mercy   6515
On him. He would die for her.
And he thought it best to leave
The court, all alone, and go
To her magic spring, and create
Such a storm of lightning and thunder,   6520
And such howling winds, and such rain,
That force and necessity would make her
Seek peace with him, or else
The spring would never be able
To stop churning out winds   6525
And rain and lightning and storms.

And as soon as Yvain felt strong
Again, cured of his wounds,
He left, and no one knew it.

But the lion went with him, who meant   6530
For the rest of his life never
To leave his companion's side.
They rode till they saw the spring,
And Yvain made the winds and the rain.
Don't think I'm a liar, please,   6535
When I tell you he made a storm
So violent that no one could tell you
A tenth of it. It seemed that the earth
Would open and the whole wood fall in.
And the lady worried for her castle,   6540
For it seemed that it too might crumble:
The walls shook, and the towers
Trembled as if ready to topple.
The bravest Turk alive
Would choose a Persian jail   6545
Rather than stay in those walls.
And all her people were terrified,
And cursed their ancestors, and said:
"Curses on the man who built
The first house in this country, and anyone   6550
And everyone who founded this town!
You couldn't find a more
Disgusting place anywhere
In the world. One man can invade us,
And torment us, and cause us such trouble."   6555
"My lady," said Lunette,
"You need to seek help! Nor
Are you likely to find anyone
Who'll help you, now that you need it,
Unless you seek it far off.   6560
I can see we'll never be safe
In this castle, we'll never dare
Go near the walls or through
The gate. You know your soldiers!

If you brought together all   6565
Your knights, there isn't one
Who'd dare come forward, not even
The very best of them! This
Is the problem: if there's no one to protect
Your spring, you'll be despised, made fun of.   6570
You'd win eternal honor,
Wouldn't you, if whoever attacks you
Gets off without a battle!
This is a desperate situation,
Unless you've made some better   6575
Plan." "You're wise," said the lady.
"Tell me what I can plan on,
And I'll do whatever you say."
"Lady! I would if I could.
I'd gladly help and advise you.   6580
But you need, and need most desperately,
Someone wiser than I am.
I don't dare interfere.
I shall endure this wind
And these rains with everyone else,   6585
Waiting, if God wills, till I see
Some brave man come
To your court, who'll assume the burden
Of this battle on your behalf.
I don't believe it will happen   6590
Today. We've not seen the worst."
But the lady answered at once:
"Girl! Talk of something different!
Don't tell me about my people,
For all I expect from them   6595
Is nothing. None of them dare
Defend the spring and the stone.
But, may it please God, let me
Hear your advice and your wisdom.

Everyone says that necessity   6600
Is always friendship's best test."
"My lady! If anyone thought
He could find the man who killed
The giant, and conquered three knights,
It would be well to go and seek him.   6605
But you heard him. As long as he bears
His lady's ill will, and her anger,
I suspect there's no one on earth
He'd follow, neither woman nor man,
Until someone swore on oath   6610
That they'd do everything they could
To end her displeasure, so bitter
And such a burden to him
That he's dying of sorrow and pain."
And the lady said: "Before   6615
You start on this quest: I'm ready
To swear, and I swear, and you have
My word, if he'll come to me here,
Without deception or deceit
I'll do everything I can   6620
To bring about this peace."
Then Lunette replied: "Lady!
It won't be easy. You may wish
To do it, it may please you to try,
But it's bound to be difficult. Still,   6625
If this is your pleasure, and you wish it,
I can take your oath before
I start on my journey." And the lady
Said: "I have no objection."
Lunette, who was always courteous,   6630
Immediately brought her an immensely
Precious holy relic,
And the lady fell to her knees.
And in all sobriety and courtesy

Lunette accepted that deceptive   ·6635
Oath. She was careful, administering it,
To omit nothing that might
Turn out to be useful. "Lady!"
She said. "Raise your hand!
I want you not to accuse me   6640
Of anything, after tomorrow.
You're doing nothing for me.
You're doing this for yourself.
Now swear, if you please, that in order
To help the Knight of the Lion   6645
You propose to exert yourself
In any way you can,
Until he has his lady's
Love again, as completely
As ever." The lady raised   6650
Her right hand, and declared: "I swear it,
Exactly as you've said: and I say,
May God and this holy saint
Help me and keep my heart
From failing; let me do all I can.   6655
If I have the strength, and I can,
I'll help him return to the love
And the grace he once knew with his lady."

Lunette had done her work well.
There was nothing she'd wanted as badly   6660
As this, and now she'd done it.
A horse with an easy gait
Was already ready. Feeling
Cheerful, with a smile on her face,
She mounted and rode off, then found   6665
Under the pine tree, the man

She'd hardly expected to find
Without riding a great deal farther.
She'd thought it would be distinctly
A longer and harder journey.   6670
She recognized the lion,
Then Yvain, as soon as she saw them,
And galloped directly toward them,
And dismounted, and stood on the ground.
And Yvain had known her as soon   6675
As he saw her, even far off,
And greeted her. And she greeted him,
Saying: "My lord, I'm delighted
To find you so near at hand."
And my lord Yvain answered: 6680
"Why? Were you looking for me?"
"Yes! And I've never been so pleased
Since the day I was born. And this
Is what I've gotten my lady
To do—unless she perjured   6685
Herself: as soon as she can
She'll be your lady and you
Her husband. I'm telling you the truth."
My lord Yvain was delighted
To hear such news; he'd never   6690
Expected to hear it. He couldn't
Stop thanking Lunette
For having accomplished it. He kissed
Her eyes, and then her face,
And said: "Oh, my sweet friend!   6695
How could I ever repay you,
What could I possibly do?
There'll never be time enough
To honor and serve you as I'd like."
"My lord!" she said. "It's not   6700
Important. Don't give it a thought!

You'll have time enough and to spare
For helping me—and others.
If I've paid this debt, which I owed you,
Then you owe me no more   6705
Acknowledgment than anyone who borrows
Anything and later returns it.
Nor do I think, still,
That I've truly repaid you what I owe."
"You have, as I stand in God's sight,   6710
Five hundred thousand times over.
And now, if you're ready, let us go.
But what have you told her? Does she know
My name?" "No, by my faith!
The only name she knows   6715
For you is the Knight of the Lion."

And so they chatted as they rode
Along, the lion behind them,
Until they came to the castle.
And they spoke not a word to anyone,   6720
Neither to a man or a woman,
Until they stood in the lady's
Presence. And the lady couldn't
Have been happier, hearing the news
That the girl was coming and bringing   6725
With her both the lion
And his knight. She longed to see him
Again, and come to know him.
And my lord Yvain, dressed
In full armor, helmet and visor   6730
And all, fell at her feet,
And Lunette, standing next to him,
Exclaimed: "My lady, raise him,

And use your best wisdom and all
Your power to bring him peace   6735
And a pardon, as no one else
In the world could possibly do!"
So the lady asked him to stand,
And said: "Anything I can do
I will do! If I possibly can   6740
I wish to procure him what he asks for."
"My lady! I shouldn't say it,"
Said Lunette, "if it weren't true.
But it's even more possible, and within
Your power, than I've told you. But now   6745
I'll tell you everything, and you'll see
How truly I spoke. You've never
Had so good and loyal
A friend as this man here.
God Himself, who wishes   6750
For peace and love between you,
Love and peace unending,
Led me to find him, today.
And to prove how rightly I speak
All I need to say is: 6755
My lady! Forget your anger!
His only mistress is you.
This is Yvain, your husband."

The lady trembled at these words,
And said: "May God save me!   6760
You've hooked me beautifully, haven't you?
You'll make me love him in spite
Of myself, though he neither loves
Nor respects me. A fine bit of business!

You've served me remarkably well!   6765
I'd rather spend my life
Buffeted by storms and wind!
And if breaking an oath weren't low
And villainous and ugly, I'd never
In all this world come to terms   6770
With him, or give him any peace.
It would have burned inside me,
Like a hidden fire smouldering
Under cinders—but I have to make peace,
So I wish to speak of it no more,   6775
Nor ever mention it again."

And Yvain heard, and understood
That things were going well,
That he'd have his peace and forgiveness,
So he said: "Lady! We ought   6780
To show pity to sinners. I've had
To suffer for my folly, and I ought
To have suffered, it was only right.
It was folly that kept me away;
I was guilty, you were right to punish me.   6785
It's taken courage to come
And stand before you. I've risked it.
But now, if you'll take me back,
I shall never injure you again."
"Surely," she said, "I'll consent.   6790
If I didn't do everything in my power
To bring peace between us, I'd be guilty
Of perjury. And now, if you wish it,
I grant you your request."
"Lady!" he exclaimed. "A thousand   6795
Thanks! The Holy Spirit

And even God Himself
Couldn't make me happier than that!"

And now Yvain had his peace,
And surely, believe me, nothing   6800
Had ever pleased him better,
However miserable he had been.
It had all come right in the end.
His lady loved him again,
And cherished him, and he cherished her.   6805
He'd forgotten all his worries,
Wiped away by the joy
He felt with his dear sweet love.
And Lunette was vastly relieved:
Nothing she'd wanted was denied her,   6810
Now that she'd fashioned an unbreakable
Peace between generous lord
Yvain and his one true love.

So ends The Knight of the Lion,
A story told by Chrétien,   6815
For nothing more's been heard of it,
And no one will ever tell more—
Unless he feels like lying.

Afterword

Joseph J. Duggan

Chrétien de Troyes wrote in the second half of the twelfth century. What little we know about him comes from the prologue to his romance *Cligés,* where he identifies himself as the author of six other works: *Erec and Enid*; a tale about King Mark and Isolt the Blonde; adaptations into Old French of Ovid's *Art of Love* and *Remedies of Love*; two stories from that same author's *Metamorphoses*—"Philomène," probably preserved as part of the thirteenth-century *Ovide moralisé,* and the lost "Bite on the Shoulder," perhaps a version of the story of Pelops.

That Chrétien was schooled in Latin is certain, and he may well have been a clerk in at least minor orders. The other romances ascribed to him with assurance, namely *Yvain, Lancelot (The Knight of the Cart),* and *Perceval (The Tale of the Grail),* are assumed to have been written after *Cligés.* Both *Lancelot* and *Perceval* are unfinished, the first because for some reason Chrétien gave it over to another writer, Godefroy of Lagny, to complete, and the second probably because he died before bringing it to a conclusion. *Erec and Enid* is thought to have been written around 1170 and *Perceval* in the decade before 1191, the year in which Phillip of Flanders, the poem's patron, died. Most scholars also take that year to mark the latest possible date of Chrétien's poetic ac-

tivity. *Yvain* was probably composed around 1177, either
shortly after or shortly before *Lancelot*. Another romance by a
writer named Chrétien, *Guillaume d'Angleterre,* is sometimes
assigned to Chrétien de Troyes, but the attribution is du-
bious. Two of Chrétien de Troyes' love poems have, however,
survived.

The town of Troyes, located southeast of Paris, was in the
Middle Ages the residence of the count and countess of
Champagne and the site of a very important fair to which
merchants from all over Europe came annually to sell their
wares. Working in such a cosmopolitan center, at a court fre-
quented by Andrew the Chaplain (author of that astonishing
treatise known as "The Art of Courtly Love"), the poet
Conon of Béthune, the romancer Gautier of Arras, the
chronicler Villehardouin, the epic poet Bertrand de Bar-sur-
Aube, and many other authors, must have exposed Chrétien
to a multitude of influences. Marie, countess of Champagne,
under whose guidance and patronage he wrote *Lancelot,* was
the daughter of King Louis VII of France and Eleanor of
Aquitaine. After her divorce from Louis, Eleanor had married
the young Henry Plantagenet, who shortly thereafter suc-
ceeded to the throne of England as Henry II. Although we
are particularly ill-informed about the relationship between
Marie and her mother, this link with the British Isles may
ultimately be responsible for the Celtic background of Chré-
tien's romances.

Yvain is such an entertaining story that it is easy to over-
look its moral tenor. From the opening lines, Chrétien in-
vokes the Arthurian milieu as an exemplary world capable of
teaching values to his contemporaries, and he contrasts the
way people loved in his own period with the ways in which
love flourished in King Arthur's day. For him the "modern"
age does not come off well in the comparison. Always look-
ing for a way to justify his own pursuits as a writer—a com-
monplace among medieval authors—he asserts that it is

better to speak of those endowed with true courtly virtues,
even if they be dead, than to waste one's time on uncouth
contemporaries. The emphasis on characters as models of con-
duct leads one to understand that the story of Yvain's adven-
tures has more than mere entertainment value. For

> Words can come to the ear
> Like blowing wind, and neither
> Stop nor remain, just passing
> By, like fleeting time,
> If hearts and minds aren't awake,
> Aren't ready and willing to receive them.
>
> [ll. 157–62]

In fact, although the hero manages to win out in the end
over the hostility of Sir Kay, the prowess of Gawain, his own
wife's quite justifiable anger, and various preternatural forces,
his demeanor in the early sections of the romance is by no
means unblemished. Indeed, beginning with his furtive de-
parture from Arthur's court, his behavior is initially quite
problematic.

Yvain's purpose in seeking out the fountain that had been
the occasion of Calgrenant's shame is praiseworthy in itself,
since he wants to avenge his cousin. But to call the latter a
fool and then set off against Kay's advice, without taking
leave of the king or telling any of his companions where he
is going—without *any* public revelation of his actions, in
fact—is conduct that hardly qualifies as courtly. That he
does not want to request from King Arthur the right to
challenge the knight of the fountain, for fear of losing the
opportunity to Kay or Gawain, does not justify his stealing
off, especially in a society in which openness of conduct was
a guarantee of its probity. Defending himself against the
knight of the fountain is a legitimate act, but he only pur-
sues the wounded Esclados to his castle in order to procure
evidence that will satisfy Calgrenant and Kay, an impetuous

decision that leads to his confinement between the sliding
blade and the gate, in an enclosure that Chrétien compares
tellingly to

> a trap
> Set for a rat when he comes
> Hunting what was never his.

[ll. 913–15]

That the charming and clever Lunette saves the hero is, on
the other hand, a gesture in repayment of his courtesy on a
previous occasion when he alone had helped her at court.
This long first section of the romance takes Yvain from King
Arthur's entourage to Laudine's castle, where the royal court
eventually comes to him. It also serves to familiarize the
reader with Yvain's courage, physical abilities, and tempera-
ment. This prepares us for the testing of his moral character
in the conflict between loyalty to Laudine and the allure-
ments of knightly fame, as Gawain entices him to depart on
a prolonged series of tournaments. The two courtly heroes are
so successful that they attract more and better knights than
Arthur himself has done, inducing the king to come to their
court rather than to await their attendance at his. Yvain's
forgetfulness and haughtiness at this stage fall into the same
category as his lack of courtesy in slipping away from court:
it is the conduct not of a bad character but of a self-indul-
gent one, lacking at times in the concern for the feelings of
others that lies at the root of courtliness.

Yvain begins to redeem himself only in the second part of
the tale, after the terrible ordeal in which he loses his senses,
tears off his clothes, and lives as a wild man in the forest—
the hermit his only contact with civilization. In order fully
to appreciate the significance of this crisis, one has to re-
member that in the Middle Ages the deep woods were not
an inviting place of repose from the hubbub of town life.
Rather, they were considered primarily as threatening, the

locus of encounter with savage beasts and with creatures that
we nowadays consider fantastic and legendary but which for
medieval society were very real. To minds accustomed to
thinking of both nature and human actions as representative
of some hidden and higher reality, the stripping of the ac-
couterments of ordinary social life from Yvain must have
symbolized a radical transformation—not just physical and,
as we would say today, psychological, but spiritual and
moral—an external manifestation of his shame. When those
trappings are restored to him by the lady of Noroison's ser-
vant, who applies to his body perhaps a little too eagerly the
unguent whose ultimate source is Morgan le Fay, he is quite
meaningfully a new man, no longer the Yvain of old whose
reputation was destroyed by his public shame, but as it were
a man without renown, with a new name to make for him-
self.

That name presents itself to him in the guise of the lion,
a sensitive beast human enough in its capabilities to attempt
suicide when it thinks its master is dead. The lion's un-
alloyed fidelity acts as an antidote to the selfish lack of con-
cern for others whose consequences drove Yvain to madness.
The beast's moral characteristics immediately begin to rub
off on his master. With each of the major adventures in the
second half of the romance—the struggle against Count Al-
ier, the defense of Lunette against her three accusers, the de-
feat of Harpin of the Mountain, the combat with the "sons
of the devil" in the Castle of Infinite Misfortune—Yvain
builds another reputation, but always under the new name of
"Knight of the Lion." When he finally rejoins Arthur's court
he is for the king's entourage another person entirely, only to
be identified as Yvain when he reveals himself to Gawain,
but at that point already marked as one of the greatest of
knights because he has proven himself to be Gawain's equal
in combat. Yvain starts, then, from relative mediocrity as an
untested and unpolished knight, rises in stature as the suc-

cessful suitor of a rich widow, then fails through his own un-
courtly behavior. After performing a series of exploits—alone,
then in the company of the lion—he finally triumphs, fight-
ing Gawain to a draw without the lion's help amid the gen-
eral admiration of Arthur's courtiers, the ultimate judges of
chivalric worth. It is noteworthy that the deeds he performs
after the balm has taken effect are progressively more disin-
terested. He first helps the lady of Noroison, to whom he is
indebted for his recovery, then the relatives of his close friend
Gawain, and finally Lunette, who is only in her predicament
because of his own failure to return to Laudine at the ap-
pointed time. But in the Castle of Infinite Misfortune he lib-
erates captives to whom he owes nothing, and his defense of
the younger daughter of the lord of Blackthorn is undertaken
"for charity and noble generosity," in spite of the fact that he
does not know the woman and she does not know him
(ll. 5987–90).

But what about Laudine of Landuc? This much-tried lady
loses two husbands in the course of the romance, although
one eventually comes back to her under what might not seem
to be the most desirable of circumstances. The gradual re-
versal of her initial feelings for Yvain is a miniature master-
piece of storytelling. The art of weaving a good tale had
never died out during the hiatus between the decline of Ro-
man civilization and the revival of learning that began to
gather force in the twelfth century. But psychological analysis
was practically unknown in narratives of the early Middle
Ages. In the earliest extant romances, written in France in
the mid-twelfth century, authors had to grapple with the
problem of representing the workings of the human personal-
ity, a process of exploration that ran parallel to renewed in-
terest in the psyche. Chrétien, who as far as we know was
the first poet to write romances about King Arthur, ex-
ploited the innovations of his predecessors in depicting the
complexities of Laudine's sentiments. The internal dialogue

in which she debates whether to admit that Yvain might
have had some justification in mortally wounding Esclados
shows her taking the part of both accuser and defendant and
coming to the conclusion she had wished to reach in any
case,

> And all the time igniting
> Herself, like smoking wood,
> Bursting into flame when it's stirred,
> Smouldering if no one blows it
> Awake.

[ll. 1777–81]

The transformation is orchestrated by the resourceful Lu-
nette, who pays for her daring but is still there at the end,
restored to favor and up to her old deceptions. Just as Lu-
nette maneuvered her mistress into a position in which she
would be receptive to Yvain's attentions, despite the fact
that he had given her husband his death blow, so here she
tricks Laudine into saying that she will procure for the
"Knight of the Lion," whom Laudine does not recognize as
her offending husband, all that he asks for.

But in her mythic past Chrétien's courtly character Lau-
dine, lady of the fountain and bestower of the magic ring of
invulnerability, was in all likelihood no simple mortal. There
is virtually universal agreement that somewhere in the tradi-
tion from which Chrétien took many of the elements of his
tale, Laudine was a fairy and her kingdom an Otherworld
realm. One of the ways that travelers enter the Otherworld in
folklore and romance is through water, and the fountain, its
wonders, and the test to which they give rise are no doubt
the frontier between two existences—a frontier that Calgren-
ant failed to merit crossing. Lunette too, with her ring of
invisibility, was once a helper-fairy, although in Chrétien's
tale her character, like that of Laudine, is much more com-
plex.

Yvain, whose role corresponds to that of the mortal held captive by the fairy so that he might defend her kingdom against intruders, has rich antecedents in the history of northern Britain and in the traditional literature, folklore, and mythology of the Celtic realms. In the medieval Welsh triads, a storehouse of traditional lore, "one of the three fair princes of the Isle of Britain" is Owein,[1] a name for which the French equivalent is "Yvain." This Owein, who appears as a character in native Welsh poetry and narrative prose, notably in *The Dream of Rhonabwy,* where he is accompanied by a flock of ravens who fight Arthur's men, was in fact a historical king of the late sixth century; he was the son of Urien of Rheged, an ancient British kingdom situated in what is now northwest England and southwest Scotland. While Chrétien's other works contain the names of numerous figures also found in Celtic sources, Yvain is one of the few to have come over into continental romance still associated with his father.[2]

Stories of Celtic provenience, what the French call the *matière de Bretagne,* owed much of their popularity in Chrétien's day to Geoffrey of Monmouth, a cleric who published in around 1136 the fabulous *History of the Kings of Britain.* This book treats King Arthur as one of a long line of British monarchs supposedly descended from Brutus, the great-grandson of Aeneas, and presents his court as a great center of chivalry and civilized conduct. Geoffrey in fact mentions Yvain under the form *Iwenus,* as the nephew of the king of

1. Rachel Bromwich, "Celtic Elements in Arthurian Romance: A General Survey," *The Legend of Arthur in the Middle Ages: Studies Presented to A. H. Diverres by Colleagues, Pupils and Friends,* ed. P. B. Grout, R. A. Lodge, C. E. Pickford and E. K. C. Varty (London: D. W. Brewer, 1983), p. 43.

2. Rachel Bromwich, ed. and trans., *Trioedd Ynys Prydein: The Welsh Triads* (Cardiff: The University of Wales Press, 1978), p. 7.

Scotland. Geoffrey's work was translated into Old French in around 1155 by Wace, who added certain attributes to the record of Arthur's achievements, including the Round Table "about which the Bretons tell many a fable." Wace also mentions that professional storytellers had already associated many wonders and adventures with Arthur. Of interest to us here is the fact that in another work, the *Roman de Rou,* Wace expresses his fascination with the forest of Broceliande in Brittany where, he tells us, according to the Bretons, fairies and marvelous adventures are sometimes encountered and where the fountain of Barenton is found, which causes rain if one pours water over the stone located beside it. Wace went so far as to visit the area but, he reports, came back as great a fool as when he went. Since the *Roman de Rou* was in all likelihood written before *Yvain,* either the legend of the magic fountain existed in tradition, from which Chrétien somehow picked it up, or Chrétien knew of it from reading the passage in Wace. In any event the fountain in *Yvain* does not appear to be situated in Brittany.

Other notable characters and features of *Yvain* have Celtic parallels: the birds singing in the trees after the storms that Calgrenant and Yvain provoke; the figure of Morgan le Fay, from whom comes the unguent that heals Yvain and who traditionally takes on the appearance of a blackbird; the lady of Noroison, whose name signifies "black bird" and who may have been herself a manifestation of Morgan in some lost source. Certain aspects of three characters—the hospitable lord of the castle with whom both Yvain and Calgrenant stay the night before they reach the enchanted fountain, the gigantic, deformed herdsman who guards the wild bulls and points the way to the fountain, and Esclados the Red—have led scholars to think that they may be narrative descendants of the giant Curoi, a sun god known to us through Irish tales but no doubt also figuring in early Welsh literature, most of which has been lost.[3] Likewise the motif of the hidden name recalls the tale in which the Irish hero Cuchulainn kills his own son in single combat. Other plot devices with folkloric sources include the pouring of water on a stone to bring rain by sympathetic magic (the copper gong in the hospitable host's castle may have the same relation to thunder) and the magic rings so useful to the hero. Still other elements may have classical sources; for example, the lion's gratitude may owe something to the tale of Androcles, and some of the comments on love appear to be based on Ovid. But *Yvain*'s major debt is to Celtic traditions.

The only written record of a realization of part of the story, prior to Chrétien, appears in the anonymous *Latin Life of St. Kentigern,*[4] written in Scotland between 1147 and 1164. Here, Ewen (= Owein, Yvain), son of King Ulein (= Urien), seduces Thaney, the daughter of King Leudonus of Leudonia, that is to say Lothian (compare Chrétien's version of Laudine's father's name, "Laudunet of Landuc"). St. Kentigern, the patron saint of Glasgow cathedral, is said in the *Life* to have been the son of Thaney and Ewen. According to the story, Ewen courted Thaney, but she refused to marry him, and in retribution her father sent her to work as the servant of a swineherd. Desperately in love with her, Ewen sent a woman to try to persuade Thaney to grant him her affection; when this failed, he disguised himself as a girl

3. For a discussion of these and other Celtic elements, see Roger Sherman Loomis, *Arthurian Tradition and Chrétien de Troyes* (New York: Columbia University Press, 1949).

4. Alexander Penrose Forbes, ed., *The Lives of S. Ninian and S. Kentigern, Compiled in the Twelfth Century* (The Historians of Scotland Series, 5; Edinburgh: Edmonston and Douglas, 1874), pp. 123–33, 243–52. See also Kenneth Hurlstone Jackson, "The Sources for the Life of St. Kentigern," in *Studies in the Early British Church* (Cambridge: Cambridge University Press, 1958), 273–357.

and met her near a fountain. Through trickery, he led her away to an isolated spot and raped her, as a result of which she conceived the child Kentigern. Ewen then abandoned Thaney. Her father punished her for becoming pregnant by having her thrown from a mountaintop, but she survived unharmed, after which a clear fountain, no doubt a token of her innocence, sprang up miraculously. Her father then pursued the swineherd into a marsh, apparently under the impression that he was responsible for the conception, but the herdsman managed to kill the king. So at least a decade before Chrétien's work the Yvain figure appeared in a story in which, in league with a female intermediary, he courted and abandoned a lady of the fountain(s) who was associated with a herdsman. Ewen's disguise appears to be analogous to Yvain's ring of invisibility. Chrétien may have been the one to link this story, or more likely—since it was probably a traditional tale taken up by the author of the *Life of St. Kentigern*—a variant version of it, with the legend of the rain-producing fountain.

Chrétien did not, then, make up the story of *Yvain* out of whole cloth. But it is not always easy to tell just which detail is traditional and which original in his romance. This question of sources may be more bothersome to us than it would have been to him, since many a medieval author took pride in the traditional quality of his story. Originality in the sense of the invention of new material was not yet a desideratum that took precedence over other considerations. What is apparent, however, is that the legendary elements from Celtic sources have been demythologized and rationalized, either by Chrétien or by his predecessors; in place of an awareness of mythic meaning, one encounters Chrétien's own concerns for courtliness, personal worth, and correctness of knightly behavior. He never tells us that Laudine and Lunette were once fairies (if in fact he knew); on the other

hand, the moral points of his tale have also to be derived
from careful reading, since overt didacticism does not appear
to have been part of his literary makeup.

A medieval Welsh tale, "The Lady of the Fountain," in
the collection commonly known as the *Mabinogion,* tells a
story that is an obvious counterpart to *Yvain.* It was once
thought that *Yvain* and "The Lady of the Fountain" derived
from a common source. It is much more likely, however, that
a reading of Chrétien's romance was heard by some Welsh
storyteller who retold the tale using elements familiar to his
audience and stripping it of most of the characteristics that
make it instructive in the ways of courtliness.[5] In "The Lady
of the Fountain" Owein does not insult the Calgrenant figure
(Cynon), nor does Arthur declare his intention of testing the
fountain before Owein's departure from court; no particular
motivation is assigned to Owein's pursuit of the fountain's
defender, and Owein makes no attempt to convince the lady
of the fountain that he loves her. He jousts for three days
with Gwalchmei (Welsh counterpart of Gawain) after he de-
feats Cei (= Kay) at the fountain, eliminating both the
need for and the potential effect of a duel with Gwalchmei
at the end of the tale. Arthur, rather than Gwalchmei, lures
Owein away from his wife, and the conflict between knight-
hood and marital obligations is greatly muted since the rea-
son for the separation of husband and wife is not so that
Owein can demonstrate his prowess in tournaments, but
rather so that Arthur can show him to the nobles of the Is-
land of Britain. Owein's reconciliation with his wife is
achieved immediately after he defends Luned, and quite
abruptly:

5. The conventional features of Welsh storytelling are discussed in
Brynley F. Roberts, "From Traditional Tale to Literary Story: Middle Welsh
Prose Narratives," in *The Craft of Fiction: Essays in Medieval Poetics,* ed.
Leigh A. Arrathoon (Rochester, Michigan: Solaris Press, 1984), 211–30.

And then Owein, and Luned with him, went to the domin-
ions of the Lady of the Fountain. And when he came away then
he brought the lady with him to Arthur's court, and she was his
wife so long as she lived. [*The Mabinogion,* trans. Jones and
Jones, pp. 180–81]

After this point Owein overcomes the Black Oppressor, in
the tale's equivalent to the adventure of the Castle of Infinite
Misfortune. The moral improvement that Yvain's character
undergoes in the increasingly selfless adventures Chrétien has
him undertake, leading up to the reconciliation, is quite ab-
sent in Owein's experiences, and the feats the hero performs
have no particular progression to them. While the Welsh tale
exhibits its own very fine qualities of vividness and color, it
differs from Chrétien's romance in tone, in a myriad of de-
tails, and in meaning, in ways that highlight the French au-
thor's preoccupation with courtly behavior.

Since Chrétien was writing for the court of Champagne,
his concerns generally parallel those of the noble class: the
behavior of knights and ladies, proper conduct in love affairs,
the duties of rulers. One of the most significant scenes in his
Eric and Enid, in fact, is the couple's coronation, during
which Erec wears a silk robe ornamented with scenes depict-
ing the quadrivium—four of the seven liberal arts (geometry,
arithmetic, music, and astronomy) constituting the school
curriculum and no doubt the arts most useful for the task of
ruling a kingdom. All the more surprising, then, that one of
the episodes in *Yvain,* the Castle of Infinite Misfortune (one
of those enigmatic "customs," as Chrétien calls them, insti-
tutionalized wonders that dot the hazardous landscape of Ar-
thurian romance, providing adventure for knights who
wander in search of it) should present a tableau of economic
exploitation—the captivity of the ladies who have been sent
as tribute from the Island of Virgins forced to weave silk day
after day for slave wages and a miserable allotment of food
while they enrich the two "sons of devils" whose tyranny

Yvain later brings to an end. The type of concern reflected
in this obviously sympathetic image of oppressed workers—
even if they are of noble stock—is unique in Chrétien's ro-
mances.

Chrétien endows his characters with a good deal of life.
The scene in which Yvain is trapped between portcullis and
gate, minus his spurs and the back half of his horse, sticks
in the mind, as does the one in which the lion humbles him-
self before his startled liberator. An ironic humor marks
Chrétien's portrayal of Laudine's indecorously rapid conver-
sion from inconsolable widow to willing bride, a conversion
engineered by Lunette, who feigns to have brought the new
husband from Arthur's court when he has been in the lady's
castle all the time. The same ironic humor marks the au-
thor's account of Yvain's hyperbolic protests of unlimited de-
votion (ll. 2025–32). There is wry comment in the contrast
between Yvain's beastly neglect of his lady and the lion's ex-
cessive fidelity—to the point of attempting a suicide that is
brought to a skidding halt only by the last-minute realiza-
tion that his master is still alive.

Chrétien has also provided certain enigmas that heighten
the reader's interest. Who is the Lady Sauvage who informs
Lunette that Arthur is seeking the magic fountain? What se-
quel can the reader imagine to the flirtatious meeting of Lu-
nette and Gawain, the one linked with the moon by her
name and the other traditionally associated with the sun?
Did no one challenge the fountain during Yvain's absence? In
the end it is not just the vividness of his narration or his
deft handling of characters but also his teasing refusal to tie
up all the loose ends and comment on all the fantastic occur-
rences that makes Chrétien's romance one of the high points
of medieval storytelling. This quality, coupled with his fre-
quent observations on the nature of love (undoubtedly of
burning interest to his immediate audience), sometimes gives
the impression that he comments a bit too much on matters

for which the modern reader might wish less explication
while passing over in silence mysteries that seem to us to cry
out for explanation.

Yvain's popularity appears to have spread quickly. Within
a generation it had been adapted into German in Hartmann
von Aue's *Iwein*. It was also translated into Norwegian in the
thirteenth century and Swedish in the fourteenth, and the
fourteenth-century English romance, *Ywain and Gawain*, de-
rives from it.

Although *Yvain* is a favorite among readers of Chrétien,
none of his other works lags far behind in quality. *Erec and
Enid* shares with *Yvain* the theme of the proper balance be-
tween the duties of marriage and the demands of knight-
hood, exploring the story of a couple who lack confidence in
one another. They find it in a series of adventures that take
them away from Arthur's court after their wedding, climax-
ing in the mysterious "Joy of the Court" episode in which
Erec delivers from enchantment a knight (Mabonagrain, ava-
tar of the Celtic god Mabon) who is the mirror image of
himself. *Cligés* also presents an Arthurian ambiance, but its
principal hero is the young heir to the empire of Constanti-
nople, which his uncle has usurped from him. Cligés regains
the throne after falling in love with his uncle's young wife,
Fénice, "the Phoenix," who refuses to commit adultery and
become another Isolt but manages through the stratagem of
a feigned death to unite herself to Cligés despite all obsta-
cles. In fact, adulterous love is the major concern in only one
of Chrétien's romances, *Lancelot,* a work that he wrote at the
request of Marie of Champagne and then relinquished before
it was finished, perhaps because he disliked the task of pre-
senting the affair between Queen Guinevere and Lancelot in a
positive light.

Lancelot begins with the evil king Melegant's arrival, one
Ascension Day, at King Arthur's court, where he issues a

challenge. He will set free those of King Arthur's subjects whom he holds prisoners if any knight is capable of defeating him in battle. But if Melegant wins, his prize will be Queen Guinevere. Sir Kay cajoles Arthur into allowing him to take up the challenge. But Melegant triumphs and leads both Kay and the Queen off into captivity, with Gawain and Lancelot in pursuit. Lancelot manages to make his way to her, overcoming enchantments and other obstacles and undergoing the ignominy of having to ride in a cart, vehicle of infamy, whence the designation "Knight of the Cart." Finally he visits the cell in which Guinevere and the wounded and unconscious Kay are imprisoned, and makes love to her. This leads Melegant to accuse Kay of having committed adultery with the queen, an accusation that is to be tested by judicial combat. Himself sequestered through the machinations of Melegant's retainers, Lancelot succeeds in freeing himself long enough to take part, incognito, in a tournament at which Guinevere is present. Here he fights alternately as poorly and as well as he can, according to the queen's command. He then returns to captivity, but escapes once again from his tower prison to kill Melegant in the judicial combat that takes place at Arthur's court.

The action of *Lancelot* is referred to on three occasions in *Yvain*. The first occurs when Lunette tells Yvain that she would have asked Gawain to defend her against the accusations of unfaithfulness leveled against her:

> But some knight
> Had stolen away the queen,
> Or so they told me. And surely
> The king was out of his mind
> To let her go anywhere near him.
> It was Kay, I think, who took her
> To meet the knight who carried
> Her off, which disturbed my lord
> Gawain so much that he's gone

To find her. And he'll never come back
Until he's found her, he'll never
Rest.

[ll. 3705–3716]

Then when Yvain asks the baron whom he later defends
against Harpin of the Mountain why he did not attempt to
get help from his cousin Gawain, he replies:

But a knight from some strange country,
Who came to that court seeking her,
Has taken the king's wife.
He could never have led her away,
To be sure, entirely by himself.
It was Kay, who so befuddled
The king that he allowed the queen
To pass under his protection.
The king was a fool, and the queen
Reckless, entrusting herself
To Kay. . . .
Gawain has gone off hunting
The villain who stole the queen.

[ll. 3918–28, 3937–38]

Finally, Chrétien tells us that when the younger daughter of
the Lord of Blackthorn arrived at Arthur's court,

it was just three days
Since the queen had come back from imprisonment,
Stolen by Melegant and held
Along with his other prisoners;
Only Lancelot had been left
Behind, treacherously locked
In a tower.

[ll. 4740–46]

These references to another romance, unique in Chrétien's
corpus, are the primary evidence that *Yvain* and *Lancelot* were
written at about the same time or even simultaneously. Chré-

tien may also be evoking *Lancelot* in order to emphasize certain differences between the treatments of love in the two works: Yvain's love for another lord's wife only occurs after the husband's decease, and while in both works love is the reward for chivalric achievements, in *Yvain* the love eventually succeeds within the bonds of marriage and the hero pointedly rejects offers of illegitimate attachments.

With respect to the treatment of love, *Lancelot* is atypical of Chrétien's works. In addition to the fact that he appears to present favorably the themes of adulterous love and the total submission of the lover to his lady—thus reflecting notions seldom found elsewhere in Old French literature proper but current among the troubadours writing in Old Provençal in southern France—in *Lancelot* Chrétien also undercuts the main characters, allowing them to act in ways that border on the ridiculous. He may have been unhappy with the plot and the interpretation presented to him by Marie of Champagne (as he mentions in the prologue), and he might even have attempted to walk a thin line between pleasing his patron and treating the subject ironically. In any case he abandoned his work to Godefroy of Lagny. Nevertheless, both the romance and the tale of Lancelot and Guinevere's liaison were popular in the Middle Ages. In the final book of the thirteenth-century Lancelot–Grail Cycle, *The Death of King Arthur,* the Arthurian kingdom is destroyed as a result of the couple's conduct, and later medieval writers, notable among them Sir Thomas Malory, continued to exploit this theme.

Undoubtedly the most intriguing of the myths that Chrétien propagated is to be found in his final work. In *Perceval* or *The Tale of the Grail* the young and naive Welsh boy Perceval sets off for King Arthur's court in spite of the apprehensions and warnings of his mother. She is stricken with anguish at his departure because Perceval's brothers were killed in battle, which caused his father to die of grief. As Perceval leaves, he turns to look back and realizes that his

mother has fallen to the ground, but in his eagerness to be-
come a knight he fails to return to find out what is wrong
with her. He succeeds in his immediate goal under the di-
rection of an experienced knight, Gornemant of Gohort, who
teaches him the skills of knighthood and also advises him
about social intercourse, counseling the impetuous boy
against asking too many questions.

One day, wandering in search of his mother and finding
himself in need of a place to stay, Perceval encounters two
men in a boat. One of these, a fisherman, directs the knight
to his castle, and that evening in the castle hall the fisher-
man, who is a king, presents him with a sword that will fail
only on one unspecified occasion. Perceval watches a proces-
sion pass through the hall, consisting of a young man carry-
ing a lance with a bleeding tip, two others carrying
candelabra, a maiden bearing a luminous golden grail (a dish
on which one might serve a fish at table) set with precious
stones, and a second maiden with a silver cutting-platter.
But because of his tutor's advice Perceval declines to ask any
questions about the grail or whom it serves, or about the
bleeding lance. The next morning Perceval finds the castle
deserted and just manages to cross the moat as the draw-
bridge rises. Returning to Arthur's court, he vows not to
cease wandering until he has found the lance and learned
whom the grail serves. Later Perceval is informed that his
mother had died as he was leaving home and that because
of his failure to turn back at the sight of her falling he was
prevented from asking questions about the grail and the
lance. If he *had* asked them, the Fisher King, who had been
wounded between the thighs, would have been cured. Five
years pass, during which Perceval does not give a thought to
his Christian religion. Then, on a Good Friday, he encoun-
ters a hermit who turns out to be his mother's brother and
who reveals to him that the Fisher King's father is also his
maternal uncle, who has lived in the same room for the past

twelve years, kept alive by what is served to him in the grail, namely a single communion wafer.

The romance of *Perceval* continues with adventures that Gawain undertakes, and it is thought that the hero himself might have been led back to the grail and lance had Chrétien finished the poem. Its unfinished state gave several other romancers the opportunity to furnish continuations, and two prologues were also added to explain the circumstances that led to the situation Perceval was in at the beginning of the romance. An impressive body of literature arose from Chrétien's *Perceval.* The grail quickly became the Holy Grail (although Chrétien said once that the grail was "a holy thing," he never applied that term to it as an epithet) and was interpreted as the vessel that Christ used at the Last Supper; the lance was represented as the weapon which pierced Christ's side while he was on the cross. Figures such as Wagner, Tennyson, and T. S. Eliot continued to exploit the Grail legend, and it has given rise to numerous interpretations, some farfetched, others plausible.

A progression in the ideals that Chrétien celebrates sets *Perceval* off from the rest of his works. In *Erec and Enid* the hero and heroine marry with a minimum of amatory preliminaries and only gain confidence in each other through a series of tests. Chrétien depicts in *Cligés* not one but two protracted courtships, and explores the complications posed by chastity with constant depreciatory references to the adultery of Tristan and Isolt. *Lancelot,* probably under the influence of Marie of Champagne, appears to extol adulterous love. The love between Yvain and Laudine evolves with due attention to the analysis of feelings, then is subjected to severe pressure in marriage, but prevails over formidable obstacles. Throughout his career, then, Chrétien is preoccupied with the relationship between knighthood and love. In *Perceval,* however, love between a man and woman, while it is treated as a theme, is secondary to the love of one's kin and the love of God.

The Arthurian romance flourished in France in the twelfth and thirteenth centuries, both in verse and in prose. These works undoubtedly responded to a need for examining the subtleties of motivation in human conduct, nuances that could not be explored in the other great narrative genres of the period. These were the epic, in which characters' motives are represented through their actions or their words but not through the analysis of their thoughts and feelings, and the saint's life, plainly limited as a vehicle for delving into worldly complexities. In the romance the heroes and heroines tend to act for themselves rather than being emblematic of their societies. They are tested in adventures that they often encounter in unexpected places, by creatures who seem to live according to a set of ethical norms different from those of the ordinary mortal and who share a knowledge that gives them a limited but threatening power over anyone wandering within their reach. The qualities upon which success depends are not so much physical agility and strength (although these do play an important role) as moral and spiritual strengths. The geography of the Otherworld is ineffable, often impermanent, and the creatures who inhabit it are elusive. Against this landscape the destinies of exemplary knights and ladies were played out for the entertainment and edification of noble audiences.

Chrétien's contemporaries speak of him in ways that make it obvious they took delight in his talents as a storyteller. We can imagine them listening to his works being read aloud— much as he depicts the scene in which Yvain comes upon a family in the Castle of Infinite Misfortune:

> And he saw a gentleman,
> Propped up on his elbow, lying

On a silken cloth, and a girl
Was reading him from some romance,
I have no idea about whom.
And in order to hear this romance
A lady had come to lie there
With them. She was the girl's
Mother, and the gentleman her father.

[ll. 5362–70]

While private reading was a normal practice in the twelfth
century, communal scenes such as this must also have been a
regular feature of castle life for sophisticated noble families.
It is a scene whose pleasures are perhaps not entirely foreign
to us today, in an age in which electronic media have made
the collective aesthetic experience once again common. To
enable us to share in the pleasure of *Yvain,* we now have the
lively and colloquial rendering of Burton Raffel. It is an ef-
fective intermediary between Chrétien and us, one that is
faithful to the tenor of the romance but embodied in unaf-
fected contemporary English, free of all traces of stiltedness
and archaism. To him one can extend the ultimate acco-
lade: a reader coming upon his translation unawares might
well think that *Yvain* had been written in English.

J. J. D.

University of California, Berkeley
    July 1986

Recommended for Further Reading

The following short list includes books particularly suitable for the student reader.

Medieval Texts

Andrew the Chaplain. *The Art of Courtly Love.* Translated by John Jay Parry. New York: Columbia University Press, 1941.

Chrétien de Troyes. *Perceval or the Story of the Grail.* Translated by Ruth Harwood Cline. New York: Pergamon Press, 1983.

Early Irish Myths and Sagas. Translated by Jeffrey Gantz. Harmondsworth, England: Penguin Books, 1981.

Geoffrey of Monmouth. *The History of the Kings of Britain.* Translated by Lewis Thorpe. Harmondsworth, England: Penguin Books, 1966.

The Mabinogion. Translated by Gwyn Jones and Thomas Jones. Everyman's Library. Revised edition. New York: Dutton; London: Dent, 1974.

Trioedd Ynys Prydein. The Welsh Triads. Edited with Introduction, Translation, and Commentary by Rachel Bromwich. Cardiff: The University of Wales Press, 1978.

Wilhelm, James J., and Laila Zamuelis Gross, eds. *The Romance of Arthur.* New York and London: Garland Publishing, Inc., 1984. (Includes William W. Kibler's translation of Chrétien's *Lancelot*).

Critical Studies

Frappier, Jean. *Etude sur "Yvain ou le Chevalier au lion."* Paris: Société d'Edition d'Enseignement Supérieur, 1969.

————. *Chrétien de Troyes: The Man and His Work.* Translated by
Raymond J. Cormier. Athens, Ohio: Ohio University Press, 1982.

Kelly, Douglas. *Chrétien de Troyes: An Analytic Bibliography.* Research Bibliographies and Checklists, 17. London: Grant and Cutler, 1976.

Kelly, Douglas, ed. *The Romances of Chrétien de Troyes, a Symposium.* The Edward C. Armstrong Monographs on Medieval Literature, 3. Lexington, Kentucky: French Forum Publishers, 1985.

Lacy, Norris J. *The Craft of Chrétien de Troyes: An Essay on Narrative Art.* Davis Medieval Texts and Studies, 3. Leiden: Brill, 1980.

Loomis, Roger Sherman. *Arthurian Tradition and Chrétien de Troyes.* New York: Columbia University Pres, 1949.

Topsfield, Leslie T. *Chrétien de Troyes: A Study of the Arthurian Romances.* Cambridge: Cambridge University Press, 1981.